WHEN DEATH TAKES SOMETHING FROM YOU GIVE IT BACK

Carl's Book

WHEN DEATH TAKES SOMETHING FROM YOU GIVE IT BACK

Carl's Book

NAJA MARIE AIDT

Translation by Denise Newman

Quercus

First published in Great Britain in 2019 by

Quercus Editions Ltd
Carmelite House
50 Victoria Embankment
London EC4Y 0DZ

An Hachette UK company

First published in Danish by Gyldendal in 2017 as
Har døden taget noget fra dig så giv det tilbage. Carls bog.

A CIP catalogue record for this book is available from the British Library

HB ISBN 978 1 78747 537 3
Ebook ISBN 978 1 78747 535 9

10 9 8 7 6 5 4 3 2 1

Translated by Denise Newman

Typeset by Kim Lykke www.lucky7.dk

Printed and bound in Great Britain by Clays Ltd, Elcograf S.p.A.

The translation has been supported by the Danish Arts Foundation

DANISH ARTS FOUNDATION

This book has been selected to receive financial assistance from English PEN's "PEN Translates" programme, supported by Arts Council England. English PEN exists to promote literature and our understanding of it, to uphold writers' freedoms around the world, to campaign against the persecution and imprisonment of writers for stating their views, and to promote the friendly co-operation of writers and the free exchange of ideas. www.englishpen.org

For Martin and Eigil
and our children

And higher, the stars. The new stars of the land of grief.
Slowly the Lament names them:—Look, there:
the *Rider*, the *Staff*, and the larger constellation
called *Garland of Fruit*. Then, farther up toward the Pole:
Cradle; Path; The Burning Book; Puppet; Window.
But there, in the southern sky, pure as the lines
on the palm of a blessed hand, the clear sparkling *M*
that stands for Mothers ......–

RAINER MARIA RILKE, FROM THE TENTH ELEGY

I raise my glass to my eldest son. His pregnant wife and their daughter are sleeping above us. Outside, the March night is cold and clear. 'To life!' I say as the glasses clink with a delicate and pleasing sound. My mother says something to the dog. Then the phone rings. We don't answer it. *Who could be calling so late on a Saturday evening?*

★

He had his green jacket on. I know because I saw it myself. He walked in the green forest, and beside him walked a tiger. He walked in the green forest, and he looked up at the leaves. I see that the light shimmers in his hair, which is the same colour as the tiger's pelt. He walks alone. He doesn't understand why he's alone. But he has his tiger. He had his tiger. He lays his hand on its strong back, and I see that he's untroubled. Now the road turns, he disappears around the bend, the path leads him deeper and deeper into the green forest. He was untroubled. He didn't know why he was alone. Beside him walked a tiger.

★

Once, I was pregnant, and I dreamed that the child inside me was a baby tiger.
Playful, soft and cuddly, with light brown eyes and a golden pelt.
That's how you looked when you were born.

*

You were delivered by C-section, and I got sick after the birth. I had the most excruciating migraine, and the staff in the maternity ward thought I was hysterical. I cried and complained. I could hardly contain myself. I could hardly take care of you. I fainted as I was rolling you down the hall in the see-through plastic bassinette. That's when they called in a nurse who was also a healer. I felt it when she sent a gush of warm energy towards me. That's what it felt like. But it didn't help. Finally, they sent me down to a physiologist. He said air bubbles had entered into my spinal cord because the epidural was not put in right. He turned me upside down and manipulated my limbs and back. They cracked and popped. I felt like an animal in a slaughterhouse. I was simply bones and meat. The headache went away and they sent me home. This was at the National Hospital in Copenhagen. It was freezing out and I was afraid you wouldn't be able to stand the cold. At home, you and your father fell asleep. I sat alone in the tiny kitchen. It was evening, dark. I got dressed and went out for cigarettes. 'I'm a human being,' I thought. 'Now I'm myself again, alone in my body.' Standing in the corner shop, I thought about how the cashier couldn't tell that I'd just had a child. It was my secret and it delighted me. You were my secret. I was twenty-five years old. I smiled at the cashier and went home through the snow-lit streets.

A secret:
Born 21 November 1989, at 2:32 p.m.
You weighed 7.2 pounds and were 20 inches long.
You were ravenous right after your birth.

A little friend

★

I wrote in my journal:
Monday, 1 May 1989 – a sunny day – I found out that, in the winter, I will give birth to another child. Little winter's child, it's so strange that you exist. I still can't feel you; my body still can't understand that you exist.

So excited to see him

Outside the March night is cold and clear

★

A night full of terror
A night so full of terror
A night so full of terror, so full of terror, so full of terror, so
full of terror, so

                              I cannot form a sentence

                              My language is all dried up

                                   ★

*I raise my glass to my eldest son. His pregnant wife and their
daughter are sleeping above us. The girl is exactly three years old.
Outside, the March night is cold and clear. We've been together
all day. We've been walking in the forest and playing with the
little one. She said many wonderful things, and had lots of fun.
We've talked about everything imaginable, and now we're sitting
at the round table in my mother's living room. To life! I say as the
glasses clink. We've eaten, and now we're drinking wine, we're
talking about my next-eldest son. How he didn't get into the
Danish Film School, although he made it to the final interview.
That was a big accomplishment. How he seems to be getting over
the disappointment, and will apply again next year. How he's still
enjoying his work as a chef. How he spends most of his free time
editing films. How we miss him. I say: I miss him. Too bad he
couldn't be with us tonight. But I can't wait to see him tomorrow,
I say. The dog barks. I talk about my youngest son. We laugh at
something. My mother tells the dog to be quiet. The phone rings. We
don't answer it. Who could be calling so late on a Saturday evening?*

Lilies of the valley, white roses.
The earth, black and damp.
The glass bells' delicate clinking to
night, to
                    night

⋆

Frederik, Carl Emil, Johan, Zakarias.

I have four sons.

Do you have four sons?

Yes.

The language, empty, hollow
White like white noise
white nights.
Bridal veil, grave cloth,
milk teeth, mother's milk

I nursed you and you ate heartily

You have a name

★

Carl: *(see earlier 1.1; now esp. dial.) adult male (compared to boy); esp: a young man who has passed boyhood but is still unmarried; adolescent.*

Emil: *boy's name, originates from the Latin word* aemilius, *meaning 'friendly'. The name Emil has roots in the Roman family name Aemilius. The family name is possibly connected to the Latin word* aemulus, *meaning 'hard-working, eager'.*

Carl Emil.

Friendly young man.

Friendly, eager young man.

Friendly, eager, hard-working young man.

We first settled on Emil only, but you were so broad-shouldered and strong that it didn't seem sufficient.

You are named after my grandfather and your father's grandfather

Your elder brother's youngest daughter is named after you: *Emilie.*

Your elder brother's daughter looks like you.

She doesn't call much attention to herself and:

Your smile is unforgettable (a beautiful shape):

You are part of your elder brother's daughter:

We are part of each other.

Are you part of me?

Yes.

*

I wrote in my journal:
8 November 1994.
Carl Emil has become calmer and more in harmony, and he
is unusually absorbed with drawing, painting, making masks,
playing with modelling clay, etc. Writes letters and words, and
has begun adding numbers and saving money. He has friends
and is hardly as shy or taciturn as he was two years ago. A
passionate boy, who still loves his dummy, a kiss, and his bed.
I kissed your hand and your hand was so cold that the
coldness crept up into my face, my head, my skull. Nothing
colder exists in the world. Not ice, snow. No fear, no anxiety,
no heartbreak as cold as your hand; your hand, which I kissed
with my warm, living mouth.

I said: *Little friend.*
You were twenty-five years old.
It was in March 2015.

It was
It was

Your young body in the coffin
The earth, black and damp

So strange that you don't exist, I still feel you

My body still can't understand that you don't exist

★

I wrote in my journal:
4 December 1989.
The little one has arrived! A fine little one. He sucks and
sleeps and is still just a small animal. I can sense that he has a
powerful personality in his own quiet way. He only cries (very
seldom), if there's REALLY a reason for it, and then he lets
you know – it resounds. But he also makes the sweetest tiny
sounds, as if he were singing.
I can say this about you: As if you were singing.
I can say: You were singing.
I can say: You sing in me.

You exuded a warmth that fascinated people. You exuded a
sensual warmth.

But you were also withdrawn, remote, shy.
But you were also full of joy.
But you were also sensitive, perceptive.
But you were also strong.

But you were also enquiring.
But you were also deeply rooted.

You didn't have much anger in you.

There was something about you that I don't have words for.
Something transparent, that made you suffer alone, in silence.
And when you cried over love, you really suffered.

You didn't call much attention to yourself

You shone.

Now that I have to describe you, my view becomes
problematic. I see you in relation to myself. I see you
in relation to my limitations. The limitations are part of
myself. Therefore, I don't see you clearly. It's not possible.
Nevertheless, I still see you clearly. Even though I don't
necessarily see you truly. Maybe I see part of you that
no one else can see. Maybe the truth about a person is
kaleidoscopic. All the views together make up a prism, which
is *you*. The word 'kaleidoscope' comes from the Greek and
means something like 'beautiful form observer'. To observe a
beautiful form, to be a beautiful observer of a form, to observe
a form beautifully, to form a beautiful observer.
I see you, *you are a beautiful form. You are a beautiful observer. I
have formed a beautiful observer: you.*

★

Once, when you were nine years old, we took a trip to the island of Frøja, in Norway. From there, we took small ferries to the outlying islands in the archipelago. It was the first time that you and I did something together alone, without your brothers. There was never time. I took a picture of you: you, lying on the ground, surrounded by blueberries and lingonberries. The sun is shining. Your eyes are shining. You look completely relaxed and happy. You're looking up at me, squinting to block out the sharp light. Your smile is unforgettable. We slept one night in the same bed in a little hotel on a little island whose name I've forgotten. That was the night before the photo was taken. When we ate dinner together that evening, we asked each other questions about our childhoods. It was as if we didn't know much about each other. As if we'd never had the opportunity to have a private conversation. There was never any time. We were like strangers trying to get to know each other. But it was a lovely conversation, very civilized and respectful. You asked me about my childhood. I asked you about yours. You said that the divorce was hard on you, and that you missed your father a lot. I was well aware of this. I admired that you could tell me about it. You sat across from me, eating chips. We sat outside with a view of a small harbour. It was cold, but we both preferred to sit outside.

★

I wrote in my journal:
20 May 1998.
Carl Emil is going into third grade after the summer holidays,

a little reserved and without many interests. But I think it's the age – wanting to be as ordinary as possible. With some time and space, he'll unfold more.

At a little hotel on a little island whose name I've forgotten, you unfolded. In the blueberry bushes, in the lingonberry bushes. With a view out to the little harbour. You look up at me.

★

I wrote in my journal:
1 November 1994.
Carl Emil, Joakim and Johan are about to go to sleep.
Suddenly, Joakim exclaims: My grandmother is watching over me; she's an angel!
She's dead, says Johan.
Carl Emil sits up in his bed: When I die, I don't want to be cremated, I want to be buried deep in the earth, in a cemetery.
The two young ones are a little confused. Then Joakim says: Um, um . . . When I'm old, I want to be roasted! He's completely serious.
Johan replies: When I'm old, *I'm* going to be reheated, yep, I am.
Then they lie down and fall asleep.

1994: Carl Emil 5, Joakim 4, Johan 3.

Joakim: your cousin.
Johan: your younger brother.

When Johan was almost four, he said: 'The soul is such a round white thing.'

★

On 21 November 2007, Carl turned eighteen, and he insisted on making dinner for all the many invited guests. There were at least twenty-five people around the table. Carl wanted to make Middle Eastern food. He'd never made an entire meal by himself before. The menu was ambitious. He gave me permission to help. We stood in the kitchen all day and most of the previous day. He made countless dishes and I was his assistant. Right before the guests arrived, we were both so exhausted that we lay down on the kitchen floor. We started laughing and couldn't stop. *You looked at me, your eyes shining.* We lay there in our party clothes on the wooden floor, laughing. It was a magical moment. *Your smile was unforgettable.* Then we got up and Carl greeted his guests. That evening, he discovered he had a talent. He could create a meal.
You could create a meal.

And you ate heartily

When you turned twenty-five years old, your grandfather made a speech for you. You, Joakim, and your friend, N, had made dinner for everyone who wanted to come.

Your grandfather made a speech for you. He said:

Today, Carl turns twenty-five. There's a silver medal

connected with twenty-five, something glistening, glittering. Twenty-five years: a quarter of a lifetime. And here he stands, like a Greek god, with his saucepans and spices.

That was 21 November 2014. Your grandfather was seventy-nine years old. It was about four months before you died.

★

I wrote in my journal:
11 February 2016.
All the spices you bought and used are still in my cabinet, and every time I touch them – smoked paprika, curry, cayenne – I think about how it wasn't long ago that you touched them with your warm living hands.

He's still enjoying his work as a chef

He worked fast – *eager, hard-working* – in the kitchen.

★

I raise my glass to my eldest son. His pregnant wife and their daughter are sleeping above us. The girl is exactly three years old. Outside, the March night is cold and clear. We've been together all day. We've been walking in the forest and playing with the little one. She said many wonderful things, and had lots of fun. We've talked about everything imaginable, and now we're sitting at the round table in my mother's living room. To life! I say as the glasses clink. We've eaten, and now we're drinking wine, we're

talking about my next-eldest son. How he didn't get into the Danish Film School, although he made it to the final interview. That was a big accomplishment. How he seems to be getting over the disappointment, and will apply again next year. How he's still enjoying his work as a chef. How he spends most of his free time editing films. How we miss him. I say: I miss him. Too bad he couldn't be with us tonight. But I can't wait to see him tomorrow, I say. The dog barks. I talk about my youngest son. We laugh at something. My mother tells the dog to be quiet. The phone rings. We don't answer it. Who could be calling so late on a Saturday evening? Then all our phones start ringing.
It's my sister calling.
My mother answers the phone.
I can hear my sister screaming.

Fortuna
Fortuna
I hate you

*

I wrote to you on 13 January 2015, two months and three days before you died:

Hi Sweetheart,

How are you? I dreamed about you last night; you fell and hurt yourself and cried. I was so upset about it in the dream. I woke up crying.

You wrote back right away:

```
Ha! I'm doing fine! I'm here, editing. I think
it's going to be a good film.
```

★

We stood in my kitchen on New Year's Day 2015. We were
speaking about your great grandfather, who died a few
years ago. He lived to be ninety-four. You loved your great
grandfather dearly and he loved you.
You said: 'I'm not afraid of death. I never have been.'
I said: 'I am. When I die, I want to be cremated. I don't want
to be down under the cold earth.'
You laughed, and said: 'I'm going to be buried. I want to be part
of the big system. I love nature, and I want to be a part of it.'
I laughed.
I said: 'You already are.'
I said: 'Well, thank God I won't have to be there for it.'

In the pocket of your green jacket, I found a little book –
Walt Whitman's poems – beautifully bound by your great
grandfather, leather-bound with gold letters. His name was
in it. My mother had passed it on to you. About nature's
atmosphere, Whitman wrote:

I am in love with it,
I will go to the bank by the wood and become undisguised and naked,
I am mad for it to be in contact with me.

The smoke of my own breath,
Echoes, ripples, buzz'd whispers, love-root, silk-thread, crotch and vine,
My respiration and inspiration, the beating of my heart, the passing of
blood and air through my lungs …

'Song of Myself'

> *Stop this day and night with me and you shall possess the origin of*
> *all poems*

When I found the book in your green jacket, you were dead. It was in March 2015.

You are singing in me.

★

Once, you sat up in an old crooked magnolia tree, hidden by the waxy pink flowers, the thick green leaves. I was sitting in a chair on the lawn, reading. It was April. I could hear you breathing and the wind blowing through the leaves. You said: 'When I get dead, I want to be buried under Grandma's magnolia tree.' You were four years old.

Stop this day and night with me

Now we shall hear about what no one wants to hear about

We planted a magnolia tree at your grave. It's the same magnolia tree that was next to your coffin at the funeral. There were also four apple trees. Flowers from your grandmother's magnolia tree adorned your coffin. And white lilacs, white roses, mirabelle plum branches, scilla. There were forget-me-nots and gooseberry branches, cherry blossoms and a bouquet of lilies of the valley, which was buried with you. I read from 'Song of Myself' at your burial. I read:

Earth of the slumbering and liquid trees!
Earth of departed sunset – earth of the mountains misty-topt!
Earth of the vitreous pour of the full moon just tinged with blue!
Earth of shine and dark mottling the tide of the river!
Earth of the limpid grey of clouds brighter and clearer for my sake!
Far-swooping elbow'd earth – rich apple-blossom'd earth!
Smile, for your lover comes.

How was it possible? It was possible. I stood up from my seat and read what was on the page. *Strength in sorrow*, they say, but that's a lie. Petrified, pure survival instinct, *beside oneself*, composed in a form of insanity. White, dead.

*

As a baby, you would sleep in the afternoon, in your pram, under the magnolia tree. In the green forest. You woke up and lay there, looking up into the leaves. You babbled, *it sounded as if you were singing*. Flickering light, rain of light through the green leaves.

I am out of my mind

★

You wrote this a few years ago
fly, fly, fly
don't push the world away
but let the wind bear you up
death, death, death,
and I found your notebooks when we were clearing out your
room, and saw that you wrote poems, and I hadn't known that
you wrote poems, and I saw that many of them were about
death, and I thought FATE, and I thought NO, everyone
writes poems about death when they're young, and I froze
just as when I kissed your hand for the last time, and the
cold made me shake, and I clung to your notebook, and I
staggered, about to faint, and there was so much I didn't know
about you, and there was a lot I knew about you, and you
wrote
Speculation, is death a union?
Død, Death, Mort, Meth
A blade in the machine of the weak.
Painful? Sleepless?
Sad? Tired?
Enjoy the fear, sour and sweet.
Life ends suddenly, remember that
Now - before you're dead.

now we shall hear about what no one wants to
                                    hear about
now we shall hear about død, death, mort, meth

(I summarize, my brain burns, I write, I call it notes:
meth means death in Hebrew
I didn't know you knew any Hebrew words
I didn't know you read poetry
I didn't know you wrote poetry
I didn't know)

you flew into death

you were naked when you

flew into death

on 14 March, at 11:13 p.m.

But before that you were full of life and you blossomed

Died on 16 March 2015, at 3:45 p.m.
You weighed 194 pounds and were 6 feet 4 inches long.

I smile at you from my bed like a white flower remembering the vanished sun

★

It's 16 March 2016, and I write:
He's been dead for one year now. The spring light is pale and
delicate. I went for a walk in the park this morning. A white
mist hung over the lawns. Birds sang.

I wrote in my journal:
30 March 1996.
He thinks a lot about things – is curious about what
everything is made of: types of metal, plastic, glass, concrete,
plaster, etc. – <u>materials</u> – and with the universe, World War II,
Hans Christian Andersen's fairy tales, 'the old days', writing,
maths, playing cards, doing magic, building. He <u>does</u> a lot,
<u>materializes</u> a lot – especially – and with great skill – drawings
and paintings – but also masks, robots out of cardboard boxes,
strings of beads, things made of clay, paper aeroplanes. And
he's stubborn, but hard-working – sticks with things until he's
content.
Satisfied.

You lived in your name

Hard-working

Friendly

I could hardly contain myself

no language possible language died with my child could not
be artistic could not be art did not want to be fucking art
I vomit over art over syntax write like a child main clauses
searching everything I write is a declaration I hate writing
don't want to write any more I'm writing burning hate my
anger is useless a howling cry *I'm loaded with bullets, no one
should come to me with their soft shit*

The first thing I wrote is undated, nearly illegible. It is written in April 2015, scribbled on a napkin. I wrote:

the magnolia exists
the magnolia exists

it sucks its nourishment from deep in the earth

it sucks its nourishment from deep in the earth

The first thing I thought about that was not you, was poems from Inger Christensen's *Alphabet*. I heard the poems, they came from within my body, as if Inger were inside me reading out loud. Her voice. That was the first time art wasn't vomit. It was a relief. All I could do was mirror the form awkwardly, sticking some words into it. I couldn't even mirror the form correctly.

The next thing I wrote was a few words in a notebook. I wrote on the last page of an empty book:

today is ninth november they dug a hole for a headstone base for carl's grave I cried all day

That was twelve days before your birthday. You would've been twenty-six years old.

I wrote in my journal:

21 November 2015.

when we were looking for a gravesite for you in the cemetery, there was a solar eclipse. when we visited your grave today, your birthday, there was a snowstorm. when I was grieving for you as if my heart were being ripped out of my chest, a blood moon, red and dark, rose in the sky. that was 27 september this year.

★

The French poet Stéphane Mallarmé never wrote a book about his eight-year-old son, Anatole, who died in 1879. He wanted to. But he could not. He wrote 202 fragments or notes. He wrote:

(2
so as not to see it anymore
        except idealized –
afterwards, no longer him
alive there – but
seed of his being
taken back into itself –
seed allowing
to think for him
– to see him <and to>

★

**I DARE NOT THINK ABOUT YOU
WHEN YOU WERE ALIVE
FOR IT IS LIKE KNIVES IN
THE FLESH**

The French author Jacques Roubaud writes in his book *Some Thing Black* about the time after his young wife died. The book was published in 1986. He writes:

I do not try to remember. I do not allow myself to evoke her. no place escapes her.

*

First dream (4 May 2015)
The whole family is together. We are in a large garden, and it's summer. My four dead grandparents are there. I've never dreamed about them before. Carl isn't there. It's as if my grandparents want to comfort me, but no one states the reason for it, and neither do I.

Second dream (5 June 2015)
I see Carl as a figure with his back turned, doing nothing. He's sitting, completely relaxed, looking out of a window. Beautiful light on his half-turned face, his hair hangs down his bare back.

Third dream (20 October 2015)
I dream I'm in jail. It turns out that it's not as bad as I thought it would be. You can go out to a garden. But there are bars on all the windows, doors and gates.

Fourth dream (26 November 2015)
Tonight, he was sitting on a step, in a stairwell. White light came in from the large windows.
'Carl?' I asked. 'Is that you? Have you come back?'

'I've got some difficulties with love,' he said. 'I need to get something, but I can't get into the apartment; I don't have a key.' I sat down next to him and grabbed his hands. I stroked his cheek. His skin was warm, he leaned against me. I embraced him. He was calm and collected. He was dignified. He had his green jacket on.

Fifth dream (6 January 2016)
I dreamed this morning that we were all waiting for Carl at an apartment. We were also waiting outside and the area was rather run-down, with benches and wrecked cars and scrap lumber, and there was a playing field nearby, where we were also waiting. We walked constantly back and forth between the apartment and the area outside, waiting and waiting. There were two rooms in the apartment. I never went in the one facing the street. Others were in there, his friends and Joakim and Johan. Once in a while, they came out, exhausted, just like when we were waiting at the hospital.
Carl never showed up.

Garden. Solace. Light. Stillness. Prison.
Garden. Light. Love. Stillness.
Dignity. Key. Waiting.

I dreamed about you last night; you fell and hurt yourself and cried. I was so upset

34

★

I am
hard on
myself
I torment
myself
it's your
mother
speaking, was
I hard
on you
did I
torment
you?

**Grief is
a
fucking prison**

there is so much that I didn't know about you, and I found
your horoscope when we were clearing out your room, I found
your horoscope, and I read your horoscope, I read *Scorpio,
Aries ascendant, moon in Virgo*, and I read:

The subjective image of your mother that emerges from your
birth chart is a bittersweet image. A cold and controlled figure.

Even though it might have looked as if your mother was
emotionally generous and gave freely of herself, you're

left with an unpleasant feeling that you were in some way troublesome and therefore unwanted.

This has had an immeasurably strong impact on you.

It is the foundation of your insecurity and lack of self-confidence.

I torment my-
self with blame
and fling myself
to the floor
screaming

I spit on astrology
but torment
myself with blame
fling myself
to the floor
screaming

I force myself to read your horoscope torment myself with your horoscope I want to talk to you about my guilt ask you if I've been hard on you have I tormented you did you feel unwanted I dash around the room crazily I howl cry I want to say to you that you never in any way never ever were unwanted but death is mute silent nothing else in the world so mute silent I am alone I hate my body that gave birth to something that has died that could not hold life in you I am alone I spit on my body I despise my flesh want to stick knives in my flesh punish my flesh death's heavy unbearable stillness

You wrote some years ago:

```
I knock
        no sound
I call out
        no sound
I scream
        no
        sound
```

```
A dark blanket on
```

```
my face
```

Mallarmé writes:

> Silent father
>   opening of thought
>
>   –
>   oh! the horrible secret
> I carry inside me
>   (what to do about it
>   –
>   will become
>   the shadow of his
>   tomb
>   not known –
>
>   –
>
>   that he must
>   die

Mallarmé's son died from an illness he inherited from his father. Maybe Mallarmé was unable to write a poetry collection about his dead son because of his guilt. The fragments are permeated with guilt.

GUILT

There was never time

Why didn't I make time?

He didn't call much attention to himself

★

It's my sister calling.
My mother answers the phone.
I can hear my sister screaming.
The blood drains from my mother's face. She can't speak. She's
deathly pale. We don't understand a thing. What? we say. What?
What is it? My mother hands me the phone. Now a man is
speaking. I thought it was my sister. It's Carl, he says, Carl is dead,
he says, Carl is dead, it's Carl. I say: What are you saying? What
is it you're saying? I become furious. I don't recognize the voice. I
ask: Who's speaking? He says: It's Martin, your ex-husband. His
voice is cold, mechanical. My eldest son begins to cry, he gets up and
the chair tips over. I scream: WHAT IS IT YOU'RE SAYING?
WHAT ARE YOU SAYING? Martin says: You need to come over

to the National Hospital now, we're at the National Hospital, you need to take a taxi now. I say: Who's at the National Hospital, why are you there, where is Carl, what are you saying? He says: You need to come now. You need to come over to the National Hospital right now, you need to take a taxi. What's happening? screams my eldest son. What's happened? I cry, I ask: But what has happened? Martin says: It's Carl.
He's fallen out of the window.

A night full of terror, a night

A cruel, cruel

Anne Carson writes about her brother and his death, in *Nox*. *Nox* means 'night' in Latin. She writes:
I fall, you fall, I have fallen, fell, a neutral verb, whence casual and casually.

*

OFTEN I STAY IN THE APARTMENT THE WHOLE
DAY I SEE THE SUN RISE I SEE IT SET I SIT IN
THE DARK I DON'T READ I DON'T WRITE I DON'T
LISTEN TO MUSIC I THINK WITH CONTEMPT
ABOUT PEOPLE WHO WRITE ABOUT DEATH AS
THOUGH FLIRTING WITH DEATH PAINTING
DEATH DEATH WALKS BESIDE US IT IS REAL IT IS
NOT CALLIGRAPHY NOT A FUCKING IMAGINED
SUFFERING IT IS REAL IT IS A WALL IT MAKES ME
FURIOUS MY SORROW MAKES ME FURIOUS FULL

OF HATE I AM FURIOUS OVER BEING ISOLATED
IN MY SORROW I HATE ART I HATE EVERYTHING
I'VE WRITTEN ABOUT DEATH IN THE PAST OFTEN
I STAY IN THE APARTMENT THE WHOLE DAY I SIT
IN THE DARK I SIT IN THE DARK I DON'T READ I
DON'T WRITE I DON'T LISTEN TO MUSIC

Mallarmé writes:

> Bitterness and
> need for revenge
> when he
> seems to protest
> ⸺
>
> desire to do
> nothing anymore – <nothing>
> to miss the sublime
> goal, etc. –

★

> And they laid him
> in the damp black earth
>
> cherry blossoms and lilies of
>   the valley
> rot on his chest
>
> the children cast

                        white roses
                              on
                         the coffin

                              ★

the phone rings

someone screams

            your child

your child   is

is the accident's

is   disaster's   is

breath's light wave

stops there

            the child

stops

and we who know this end

are familiar with the pain

in a stranger's look

★

Plato recounts, in *Phaedo*, the last day of Socrates' life.
Socrates has been sentenced to death and will be poisoned
by hemlock that evening. *Phaedo* is a conversation between
Socrates and a few of his friends and students, and the
conversation is about the nature of death, the afterlife, and
what philosophy is.

Socrates says:

So it appears that when death comes to a man, the mortal
part of him dies, but the un-dying part retires at the approach
of death and escapes unharmed and indestructible.

And Socrates says:

For [the soul] takes nothing with it to the next world except its
education and training; and these, we are told, are of supreme
importance in helping or harming those who have died, at the
very beginning of their journey to the other world.
Socrates says this at the end, after spending a long time
explaining how, philosophically, it's possible that the soul
retreats from death.

*

Your friend B saw in a dream that your soul was intact.
Your soul had left your body when it could tell that the body could
no longer live.
Therefore your soul couldn't understand what had happened.
Therefore your soul was confused.
That was your friend B's dream.
It was a shamanistic dream.
It was a dream journey.
Your friend asked to see, in a shamanistic dream, where you were.
You walked in the green forest with a tiger. You had on your green jacket.
It was your soul that walked in the green forest.
That was your friend's dream.

A week before you died, you went on your first shamanic
journey, your first dream journey. Your grandfather guided
you. Since I was a teenager, we have travelled in this way in my
family, because my father was into it in the 1980s. Shamanism
can be used for a lot of things. We used it especially for
healing, both mental and physical. Once, when your elder
brother was still a boy, he had a huge cluster of warts on his
hand. My father helped him find the animal that could remove
the warts. It was a rat. During a dream journey, your elder
brother saw a rat biting off the warts. The next morning, all the
warts fell off in the sink as he washed his hands.
Your friend B trained as a shaman a few years ago.
When I was pregnant with you, I saw that you were a baby tiger.
A week before you died, you went on your first shamanic journey.
You saw that your totem animal was a tiger.

Mallarmé writes:

                              (2
      transfusion —
            change in the manner
              of being, that's all

                                        I think about how
                                        rotten your body is
                                        now
                                        How destroyed
                                        How fragile
                                        How dead

                                        *He lies down in
                                        the earth rotting*

But before that he was full of life and he blossomed

                                        *I remember
                                        the vanished sun*

You didn't think about death when you died. You didn't think
about dying when you died.

But do I know that, do I know that?

                                              a perishable body

I read Emily Dickinson. On the back of an envelope, she has written:
+ that   one has
  died –
+ consciousness
  of this.
+ lone some
  place – secret
  place
+   look
  squarely
  in the Face.

A secret

*

I wrote in my journal:
10 November 2015.
Carl is very much alive, very close to me. He is like a wheat field. The stalks blowing in the wind. Golden, strong and ripe.

9 December 2015.
In the weeks after 9 November this year, meaning, the first day I began to write again, although no more than a few words, I started to feel his presence strongly. I have not felt him during the last few weeks. Where is he? Nowhere. The question asserts itself all the time, but there is no answer. I'm afraid I'll forget him. Forget the sensation of his body, his voice, his laughter. I'm afraid that he will disappear from me more and more

each day. That he will disappear in step with my healing. It's
unbearable. And maybe the only way for me to heal.
Can I feel Carl's small arms, can I feel the sensation of him as
I nursed him, slept next to him, held his hand? No. Yes. And
the sensation of holding his hand as an adult. But then it turns
into the sensation of holding his hand as he lay in the hospital.
I looked at his hand. I saw his child's hand in the adult hand.
It was bruised; he had hurt himself. I caressed his warm skin.

*I dreamed about you last night; you fell and hurt
yourself and cried*

And I wrote:
It's his spirit I feel now. He is like a huge bird or, no – his
presence is heavy and strong. And also light and springy. Yes,
springy. He is standing behind me, he puts his arms around
me, his long hair and bare chest.

Mallarmé writes:

> (1
> what do you want, sweet
> adored vision –
> who often come
> towards me and lean
> over – as if
> to listen to secret [of
> my tears] –
> to know that you are
> dead
> – what you do not know?
> – no I will not

tell it
to you – for then you
would disappear –
and I would be alone
weeping, for you, me,
mingled, you weeping for
                    child
in me
        the future
man you will not
be, and who remain
without life or joy.

I only felt you when I was out in the fresh air.
I almost never feel you anymore.
Perhaps my crying has told you that you are dead.
Perhaps you have arrived.

We gave you a coin for the ferryman

Your young body in the coffin

We say: He is part of nature now, as though it
were a comfort

★

The Polish poet Jan Kochanowski wrote *Laments* in 1580. The nineteen elegies are about the loss of his youngest daughter, Urszulka, when she was two and a half years old. It was the first time in Polish literature – in fact, in all of Eastern European literature – that a poet focused on earthly life. Poetry was for kings, heroes, the gods, God. And he wrote about losing his own child, a daughter no less . . . Such things were frowned upon. *Laments* was met with contempt and coldness. Today, Kochanowski is acknowledged for practically inventing Polish poetry. He writes:

Wherever you may be – if you exist –
Take pity on my grief. O presence missed,
Comfort me, haunt me; you whom I lost,
Come back again, be shadow, dream, or ghost.

> **Spirit,** *n.* **1.** *a. The animating or vital principle in man (and animals); that which gives life to the physical organism, in contrast to its purely material elements; the breath of life. In some examples with implication of other senses. b. In phrases denoting or implying diminution or cessation of the vital power, or the recovery of this. Also transf., lifeblood. c. In contexts relating to temporary separation of the immaterial from the material part of man's being, or to perception of a purely intellectual character. Chiefly in phr. in spirit. d. Incorporeal or immaterial being, as opposed to body or matter; being or intelligence conceived as distinct from, or independent of, anything physical or material.* **2.** *A person considered in relation to his character or disposition; one who has a spirit of a specified nature: e.g.. with preceding adjs. moving spirit.*

Inger Christensen writes in *Butterfly Valley*:

And who has conjured this encounter forth
with peace of mind and fragments of sweet lies
and summer visions of the vanished dead?

My ear gives answer with its deafened ringing:
This is a death that looks through its own eyes
regarding you from wings of butterflies.

The Greek word for 'butterfly' is 'psyche', which also means
'soul'. And so, when Socrates speaks about the soul, the
butterfly follows along. A beautiful shadow fluttering inside
the word 'soul'.

Metamorphosis
Transformation

....

I could not
write
not

breathe

I find a note you wrote shortly before your death. It says:

```
Ragnar Kjartansson: The Visitors (2012)
Life, loneliness, communion in death.
We are alone in our bodies.
```

I'm sitting on the floor with your papers and notebooks spread
out around me. I'm surrounded by your handwriting. I find
a list of 118 films you've seen, including your notes for every
one of the 118 films. I find your notes from the film school in
New York, I find the notes for the films you've edited. I find

your poems. I find an account of your modest income and modest expenses. The combination to your bicycle lock. A plan for what you need to edit in November and December 2015. A stack of drawings. A stack of drafts for the application to the film school in Copenhagen. You write:

Ever since I was a child, I have loved to
collect things (often physically). And I
have always loved stories. Therefore, it has
felt very natural to begin to edit films. The
process of taking the raw material through to
refined edits is incredible because the work
changes form many times as the puzzle pieces
fall into place.

Like writing poetry.
Like approaching the impossible: to write about you.
Small steps.

The work changes form many times

As the puzzle pieces fall into place

Not during.

I can say this about you: You were thorough.
I can say this: You were methodical.
I said at the funeral: *He had a poetic spirit.*

★

I wrote in my journal:

Carl Emil in school:

March 1997: First grade. Can <u>almost</u> read. Still incredibly good at drawing. Very extroverted and <u>clearly</u> his own person. Incredibly sweet and curious.

August 1997: <u>Reading</u> better. Still really good at maths. <u>Is</u> introverted, but much less so than before. A sensitive and strong boy with many talents – and with a *photographic memory* . . . Responsible, organized, well-mannered and active – both physically and mentally.

December 1997: Reads <u>almost</u> fluently now. <u>Much</u> better. Thriving, getting so big!

June 1998: Reading a lot. Taking fencing lessons and is exceptionally good at it. <u>Elegant</u>. Very bonded with his father.

I can say this about you: You read a lot; you were a passionate *reader*.

I can say: You had a fine collection of books.

I can say: The last year of your life, you primarily read religious texts. You read the Koran, you read the Bible, you read the Torah, you read *The Tibetan Book of Living and Dying*.

I can say: You loved your father.

I can say: You loved us.

We still feel your love.

> *Extroverted*
> *Introverted*
> The movement between poles
>
> That which finds itself between
> two poles

I wrote in my journal:

9 February 2016.

Joan Didion writes about her daughter's things in *Blue Nights*.
Her dead daughter's small blue dresses from childhood,
drawings, photos. I have none of that. Everything was burned.
Three days before Carl died, we found out that all of our
belongings that we were storing in Denmark had burned. The
entire warehouse had burned down. Everything. My books,
letters, handwritten manuscripts. I had taken only a few things
with me when we moved to Brooklyn. I have nothing to attach
my memories to, nothing to help me remember. No photos
from Carl's childhood. That's why I am afraid to forget.

The photo of Carl in the lingonberry and blueberry bushes
also burned.

Emily Dickinson writes:

 But are not
all facts Dreams
 as soon as
we put
 them behind
us –

Carl wrote to me: It's just dead things, Mum.

Taking the raw material through

*We don't understand a thing. What? we say. What? What is it? My
mother hands me the phone. Now a man is speaking. I thought
it was my sister. It's Carl, he says, Carl is dead, he says, Carl
is dead, it's Carl. I say: What are you saying? What is it you're
saying? I become furious. I don't recognize the voice. I ask: Who's
speaking? He says: It's Martin, your ex-husband. His voice is cold,
mechanical. My eldest son begins to cry, he gets up and the chair
tips over. I scream: WHAT IS IT YOU'RE SAYING? WHAT
ARE YOU SAYING? Martin says: You need to come over to the
National Hospital now, we're at the National Hospital, you need to
take a taxi now. I say: Who's at the National Hospital, why are you
there, where is Carl, what are you saying? He says: You need to come
now. You need to come over to the National Hospital right now,
you need to take a taxi. What's happening? screams my eldest son.
What's happened? I cry, I ask: But what has happened? Martin
says: It's Carl.
He's fallen out of the window.
It's Carl, I'm crying and shouting to my mother and my eldest son,
he's fallen out of the window, he's dead, we need to take a taxi, he
said, we need to take a taxi, we need to go to the National Hospital.
The phone slips out of my hand, I throw myself screaming on to the
floor, and so does my eldest son. We howl like animals. My father,
who had gone to bed a long time ago, is standing in the doorway.
My mother must have told him that we need to go to the National
Hospital. Let's go, he says. My mother says: Remember your phone.
We go out to the car, my mother, staggering, grips my hand. My
eldest son stays home with his wife and daughter. We drive off. It's
midnight. I'm screaming in the back seat. I smoke a cigarette. My
mother says: There, there, my sweetheart, oh, my little friend. My*

body lashes around the back seat. My brain is on fire. There are
no other cars on the highway. My father drives too fast. It takes us
an hour to get to Copenhagen. What? I'm thinking. What is this?
What's going on? It's as if I'm dreaming. I'm freezing, shaking. It's
as if all the life is draining out of me. Then I begin screaming again,
as though it's coming from a deep, primitive state, it's not my voice,
and the voice I hear scares the hell out of me. The sound nearly
can't come out, I can hardly breathe. I've become someone else.

★

C. S. Lewis writes, in *A Grief Observed*:

No one ever told me that grief felt so like fear. I am not afraid,
but the sensation is like being afraid.

Panic like a geyser inside the body   shoots its poison-water
                    up
                         from underground   to
the reptilian brain

★

I write sweet violet, I write fritillary, I write your brown eyes. I write
snowdrop, I write fern-green, I write you, my beautiful child. I write
enigmatic you, little sun, my child under the earth's crust. I write
the full moon rises in the night-blue sky, my heart is sick, my grief is
white.

I'm sitting on the floor surrounded by your handwriting, and, in a bag containing all the letters you've received over your lifetime, I find fifteen photos. They're the pictures you took at nine years old, when we were in Norway together and visited, among other things, that tiny island whose name I've forgotten. I'm sitting on the floor and it's ten days after I wrote about our trip. The first fourteen photos have no people in them. There is the sea, cliffs, green grass, small red wooden houses, boats and a harbour with shacks and a little ferry and white lamblike clouds in the light blue sky. I begin to cry. Why am I crying? I put the photos away. For several days, I can't figure out why those particular photos made me cry. Then I realize it's the absence of people that made me cry. As if the people had disappeared, as if all human life had been sucked out of the scenes. One morning, I take out the photos again. I find the fifteenth photo. It's of you, nine years old, on the aeroplane. Full of life. On the way to Norway with me. Your front teeth are new and jagged. You're looking straight into the camera.

★

I wrote in my journal:
21 October 2005.
Carl picked up Zakarias from kindergarten and brought him to the playground, where they made campfire bread and ate it with strawberry jam. Carl is an angel, and Zakarias worships the angel Carl.

I was lying awake all night, staring out into the dark, when suddenly it seemed like the dark was full of white shadows, white veils moving in and out and in between each other, almost like a dance, it was organic, it seemed like another dimension had materialized in the dark, I closed my eyes and opened them again, and the white shadows or veils were still there, dancing energetically, the movements had a strong peculiar energy, in and out and in between each other, in and out and in between each other, there was a faint whistling sound, it was like looking through a crack into another form of existence, I lay awake all night until it became light and the white material was sucked away, vanishing into the light, I've never seen anything like it since that night

the soul is such a round white thing

★

I don't know if at any other point in my life I've been interested in seeing a healer. I've never met or sought one out since that time in the maternity ward with you. I sought one out again because I wanted someone to heal me of my sorrow. I wasn't looking for someone who sees sorrow as a project to complete. I didn't want to take it on as a project. I didn't want to partake in treating sorrow as a project. The idea of sorrow as a project to complete disgusts me. The idea of sorrow as a project to complete in order to be well again makes me furious. I had no energy to work. I wanted someone to stroke my cheek and soothe me. I wanted care, not work. I wanted someone to lift the sorrow off my chest, if just for a moment. I asked the healer to lift the sorrow off my chest, just for a moment. She laid her hands on my chest. She said she would open my heart. Her hands sent a strong warmth there. Sorrow cannot be cured.

I've been crowned
Queen of Grief
Sorrow Mother
My throne is the dark's
Deep funnel

No one dare follow me
Into the dim halls

★

The Visitors (2012) is a video installation by the Icelandic
artist, Ragnar Kjartansson. It comprises nine separate films,
taken at Rokeby Farm in the Hudson Valley, New York, a
beautiful run-down estate from 1815. The work documents
the performance of a piece of music written and arranged by
Davíð Þór Jónsson and Kjartansson. The title refers to the pop
band ABBA's final album, and the lyrics are based on a poem
by Ásdís Sif Gunnarsdóttir.

Kjartansson brought together seven friends, most of them
musicians, from his hometown of Reykjavík. The musicians
are filmed separately, so that each film – except for one –
shows one of the participants, each in a different room of the
house. When all the shots are combined, the performance
emerges as a composed work, with both audio and visuals.

I saw this piece with Carl at Courtesy Luhring Augustine, a
gallery in Chelsea, New York, in 2013. We both were moved
by it. During the sixty-four-minute duration of the piece, we

walked around the screens, listening and watching, continually finding new structures and stories. The piece can be experienced in vastly different ways, depending on the order – whatever sequence people choose to watch the films in. One song plays over and over during the sixty-four minutes. There is something meditative about *The Visitors*. And deeply moving.

A few days later, Carl went back to the gallery to see the piece again.

Ásdís Sif Gunnarsdóttir writes:

> A pink rose
> In the glittery frost
> A diamond heart
> And the orange red fire

And she writes:

> You've taken me
> To the bitter end

And she writes:

> There are stars exploding around us
> And there is nothing, nothing you can do

*

I wrote in my journal:
10 March 2016.
I visited the healer again today, and the healer received the
'information' that Carl, at least in two previous lives, died
young. She thinks it's always been his soul's plan. 'He's a soul
who comes to help, and then leaves.' Does he leave when
he thinks he's not needed anymore? If so, then he's made a
mistake. He is needed. Last night, I had to get out of bed
and go into the living room. Wild sobbing. I sat naked in a
chair in the dark, crying with the same force as in the car on
the way to the National Hospital. Again, that strange voice
that pressed out of my body with great difficulty. I have been
physically unwell lately. Extreme exhaustion, feverish, and
today, a headache. I have an appointment with the cardiologist
tomorrow. I'm suffering from a rapid and irregular pulse.
Maybe it's my metabolism. More likely, it's from uneasiness
and anxiety.

Sorrow mother
in your naked apparel
the terrible skin
fever sore
strange
can't be in
skin room
light night
life nothing

A broken heart
A heart, which is shattered
The medical diagnosis:
Takotsubo cardiomyopathy.

I think about you all the time
and there are moments when I don't think about you. it's not a contradiction.
I carry you with me always, including when for a moment or longer I'm not
thinking about you. when I think of you with sorrow when I start thinking
about what happened to you everything in my body sinks. it's a feeling of
heaviness from the cells in the body being forced down to the earth. this feeling
doesn't seem to change over time. I'm getting better at holding back the tears if
I have to. I'm able to stop crying now for as long as one week. this is my record.
I think about you all the time and I don't think about you all the time I am able
to forget and laugh and eat and sleep I'm capable of living I'm indomitable I
carry you with me always. in this way nothing has changed

C. S. Lewis writes:

There are moments, most unexpectedly, when something
inside me tries to assure me that I don't really mind so much,
not so very much, after all. Love is not the whole of a man's
life. I was happy before I ever met H. I've plenty of what are
called 'resources'. People get over these things. Come, I shan't
do so badly. One is ashamed to listen to this voice but it seems
for a little to be making out a good case. Then comes a sudden
jab of red-hot memory and this 'commonsense' vanishes like
an ant in the mouth of a furnace.

★

I often hear that voice: I *have* understood it: Carl is dead. That's the way it is. Life goes on. And then, two hours later, I cry on the apricot marmalade, because I remember how much he loved orange marmalade, and because he received a jar of orange marmalade from my mother a week before his death. I found it in his kitchen, half eaten, when we cleared out his apartment. The maelstrom, as Didion describes in *The Year of Magical Thinking*: a little scrap of memory leading you back to the past, the time before your sorrow. My version of the maelstrom always leads forward into sorrow. Apricot marmalade turns into orange marmalade, and the marmalade leaves a sticky trace that pulls everything with it. Sweet memories of Carl turn bitter and intolerable, because they lead forward to his death.

*

I BELIEVE IN NOTHING, NOT IN HEAVEN, HELL, GOD, HEALING, PAST LIVES, I SPIT ON ALL FOOLISH NOTIONS, I DON'T BELIEVE IN HADES, THE LAW OF KARMA, AFTERLIFE, TRANSMIGRATION, I SPIT ON ALL OF IT, I RAGE WITH THE DEEPEST CONTEMPT, I DON'T BELIEVE IN FATE, ASTROLOGY, CONTACT WITH THE DEAD, GHOSTS, ANGELS, I VOMIT OVER ALL OF IT, I SCREAM FULL OF THE DEEPEST CONTEMPT, I SAY FUCK THAT SHIT, THERE'S ONLY LIFE AND DEATH, LIFE AND DEATH, I ONLY BELIEVE IN GENTLENESS, WHEN WE CARE FOR THE DEAD BODY, WHEN WE ARE FORCED TO PART WITH IT; THE COMMUNITY

At the end of September 2015, I travelled around the US alone. I was on a two-week book tour. I held it together, I managed, I *willed myself*. There was something freeing about always being on the move. It suited my state of being: constantly drifting forth, fluttering, departing, not belonging anywhere. The anonymity of being a traveller suited me; no one knew me, and no one knew of my grief. Like when I snuck out into the winter darkness to buy cigarettes after coming home from giving birth to Carl. This trip took place many months before I began to write a single word. When I got to Houston, my last stop before returning home, I visited the Rothko Chapel. It's considered to be the artist's most important work. He made all fourteen paintings, some huge and some triptychs, between 1964 and 1967. The chapel was finished in 1971, the year after Rothko's suicide. The building is octagonal and its form resembles a Greek cross. Viewed from the outside, it's grey, closed off and massive. Rothko's paintings are black, matt black, violet black, reddish black, and are created using a special technique. For the black and reddish-black paintings, he first applied red pigment, and after that, seven different dark and black shades. They're all mixed with raw egg, oil-based paint, turpentine and resin. The blackish-violet paintings also have many layers of pigment, mixed with a warm rabbit-skin glue, which makes the layers of colour transparent and light. Consequently, some areas of the paintings appear light grey and white. As the light changes during the course of the day, the appearance of the paintings keeps shifting.

The chapel is exceptional because it isn't associated with any specific religion. It's for everyone, believers and non-believers, Christians, Muslims, Jews, Buddhists, atheists, Hindus and so on – it's for all people on earth. There's nothing in the chapel except Rothko's paintings and a few wooden benches placed around the room. In a side entrance, the sacred texts of different religions are set out on a table. Rothko was not religious. People come here to meditate, pray, grieve, relax. And they come to see Rothko's work. I sat down on a bench and looked at the paintings. I sat there for two hours. After the first glance, shapes gradually began to emerge. I saw birds, the sea, fish. I saw skulls and faces. I saw trees and clouds. A long row of people bent over. And then I saw Carl. Half-turned away, his long hair down his back. I wanted to crawl into the painting to him. Then he disappeared, and I saw the moonlight, deer and turtles. Giant flowers, their whiteness vibrating in the similarly vibrating darkness. I could not stop crying. But it was a welcome cry after many weeks of suppression. It had been necessary to suppress my tears to do the book tour. I needed to cry. I got up and went out and started looking at the books that were set out. I picked up *The Tibetan Book of Living and Dying* and opened to a page at random and read the section, 'The helplessness as you observe your living family'. It is about how the dead are unable to make contact with the living. I went out into the sunshine, out in the Texan heat, walking across the lawns, I cried and cried. I said to myself: Get a grip. Stop. Stop crying. You've got to give a reading tonight, you can't show up with a tomato face and ugly swollen eyes. Stop. I was thinking the figures that emerged from Rothko's paintings reminded me of how one might see while hallucinating.

When I got home, I saw that Carl had dog-eared that exact passage in *The Tibetan Book of Living and Dying* when he'd ploughed through it while staying with us in New York. 'The helplessness as you observe your living family'. I was thinking that it's we who are helpless, because we cannot hear our dead. I read that, according to the book of death, you become part of the wind, after going through several stages of becoming a soul.

Are you part of the wind?

★

It's Carl.
He's fallen out of the window.
It's Carl, I'm crying and shouting to my mother and my eldest son, he's fallen out of the window, he's dead, we need to take a taxi, he said, we need to take a taxi, we need to go to the National Hospital. The phone slips out of my hand, I throw myself screaming on to the floor, and so does my eldest son. We howl like animals. My father, who had gone to bed a long time ago, is standing in the doorway. My mother must have told him that we need to go to the National Hospital. Let's go, he says. My mother says: Remember your phone. We go out to the car, my mother, staggering, grips my hand. My eldest son stays home with his wife and daughter. We drive off. It's midnight. I'm screaming in the back seat. I smoke a cigarette. My mother says: There, there, my sweetheart, oh, my little friend. My body lashes around the back seat. My brain is on fire. There are no other cars on the highway. My father drives too fast. It takes us an hour to get to Copenhagen. What? I'm thinking. What is this? What's going on? It's as if I'm dreaming. I'm freezing, shaking. It's as if all the life is draining out of me. Then I begin screaming again, as though it's coming from a deep, primitive state, it's not

my voice, and the voice I hear scares the hell out of me. The sound nearly can't come out, I can hardly breathe. I've become someone else. And it's raining when we get to the National Hospital, we take the lift up to the tenth floor, I step out of the lift and scream: Where's my child? Where's my child? and my ex-husband, Martin, comes out of the waiting room and tries to calm me down, he's mechanical and cold, I scream: Where's Carl? he takes hold of me, he holds me tightly, we walk down a hall, we go into an office, some nurses are sitting there, behind the office is a room, we go into that room, Carl is lying there, the first thing I notice is his eyes, they're black and blue, violently swollen, two dark arches, his eyes are closed, his lips are slightly parted, and there's a wheezing sound, it's the respirator that is wheezing, it's breathing for him.
He's alive.

★

Roubaud writes:

This image again for the thousandth time. with the same insistence. can't help replaying forever. with the same keen details. I don't see them diminish.

I wrote in my journal:
12 January 2016.
It's grey today, there's a hush in the living room. Death is something we now live with every day. I have no idea how I'll be able to put all my energy once again into writing. It demands so much energy. So much presence, concentration and energy. Beauty has abandoned my language. My language walks in mourning clothes. I'm completely indifferent.

Roubaud writes:

To cling to death as such, to recognize it as a real hunger, has meant admitting that there is in language, in all of its constructions, something over which I have no control.

★

I wrote in my journal:
30 March 1996, evening, bunk beds, Carl Emil, six years old, says:
'The sun is a kind of star, and the star, a kind of sun. But when you die, you can't get human skin and human hair again.'

I stroke his warm skin

I have a thick lock of your hair in a white envelope. Some of it is stiff with dried blood. It was clipped before the coffin was closed. It still smells like you. I was afraid that it would rot, but the blood hasn't rotted. I placed it in an envelope so that some air would get in. I divided your hair with your father. We've shared a lot in our lives – love, time, children, objects, a divorce. That we would share your hair was completely absurd. I divided it indifferently, crying, as though being whipped. Neither of us could bear the sight and smell of your hair. It was dead material even when it was growing from your scalp. Hair is dead cells. Now it seems alive. A part of you, a part of your body. It has the same bronze-gold colour as always. It smells like the sea and honey and warm spices and a little bit metallic. I think it's the blood that gives it the metallic scent. In Victorian times, people made elaborate jewellery from the deceased's hair.

Hair: *A filament structure that consists of a special form of keratin, which is formed by cell division, and keratinization of the cells in the lower section of the hair follicle.*
Hair follicles are formed in the foetus by a surplus of cells growing pin-shaped down into the skin and forming a follicle structure. After birth, no more hair follicles are formed.

Roubaud writes:

I did not save you from the difficult night.

★

In June 2015, your elder brother digs four holes at my mother's house. He plants the four apple trees from your burial in a square. He says: 'If anyone had told me three months ago that I'd be constructing a memorial for my little brother, I would not in my wildest dreams have believed them.' It's a bright summer day, and the work is heavier than the earth itself. Your big brother's elder daughter, three years old, waters with her little watering can when the work is completed. She says: *Carl lives in heaven now, and we can't visit him there.*

and we pull all the apples off the branches while they're still small so the tree
can grow strong, without the branches breaking
and we scatter blood meal around the trees to keep the deer away from the
saplings
and we stand paralyzed, gazing at the blooming trees in may
and we'd do anything in the world to keep life in these trees
we can't bear it when plants and trees die

we can't bear the thought that our mistakes and inattentiveness can cause plants and trees to die

In June 2016, your father and I drive your elder brother and his eldest daughter to a small ferry dock. They're going to sail across the fjord. We stand and watch them sail away. We wave. We get back in the car. We speak about how it's going. I say that I've felt so quiet and heavy for a long time. I say there's nothing I want. I say I'm still drinking too much. Your father says that he's felt so quiet and heavy for a long time. He says there's nothing he wants. He says he's still taking tranquillizers. That's how it goes after shock turns into silence. Into nothing. Into no-time. We're happy that it affects us in the same way. 'Happy.' We both had thought that there was something wrong with us, that no one else experienced it like us. But we experience it in the same way. Like us.

*

I wrote in my journal:
St John, 30 December 2009.
Carl arrived from Denmark on the 22nd. We flew to St Thomas on the 24th, very early in the morning. Then took a boat here. We're having a wonderful time. Salt Pond was especially beautiful, with its coral and sea plants extending all the way into the shallow water, so that Zakarias, who's a cautious snorkeller, could admire the bright blue, purple and orange fish, the sea stars and mustard corals. We had the beach to ourselves, and we climbed up to Ramshead, where slaves once fled, trying to swim to the British-owned islands, when England (before Denmark) abolished slavery. Cacti with red

flowers were everywhere, countless butterflies, flowers and bees. Today we walked in tropical rain, in the forest – along the Reef Bay Trail on the island's southern coast – and saw ruins of several old sugar plantations and a village that, until the 1940s, had been buried in the wilderness. We saw the slaves' quarters and felt deep sorrow. Carl laid his hand on the uneven rubble and said: 'Let's take a minute of silence for those who suffered and died here.' All the paths in the area are made of volcanic rocks, which the slaves hauled and set in place. Halfway down the side of the mountain was a very spiritual place: a little freshwater lake with a waterfall, encircled by wild orchids. And along the cliffs that rise up around the lake are petroglyphs from around 3,000 years ago, carved by the people who originally lived here, the Taíno tribe. The drawings reflect in the water, symbolizing the two worlds: the physical and the spiritual. But then Carl fell, he slid in the mud and cut his shin, the skin tore, blood poured out and he got dizzy, was pale and in pain, and couldn't even stand on his leg. What should we do? How would we get him up the mountain? What luck amid the unluckiness: a moment later, a small group of people comes walking up the path, being led by a doctor! He examined Carl's leg and said that it wasn't broken or sprained. We put ice on it (from our lunchbox). We said: 'Carl, you're always so lucky, what are the chances of a doctor arriving deep in the rainforest, just when you need help?'

Carl *is* always lucky.

★

You shouted: 'I DOT DE PAUER!' meaning: 'I got the power.' You were three years old and you walked in the green forest and cut down cow parsnip with a stick. You grew. You were invincible. You were strong. You climbed the highest trees, you walked on tightropes, you stood on your head, your handsprings were amazing. You could do anything with your body. You had no fear. You preferred squatting on chairs to sitting on them. When you got up, it was as if an invisible magnet were pulling you upward. You hopped down to the floor. Quick, confident. And there you stood. Straight, perfectly symmetrical. The same when you were grown up.

A perfect body.
An awareness of the body's possibilities.
An awareness of space and time.
A natural ability to use and place the body in space and time.

To overestimate your own abilities

Your handsprings were amazing

★

It's raining when we get to the National Hospital, we take the lift up to the tenth floor, I step out of the lift and scream: Where's my child? Where's my child? and my ex-husband, Martin, comes out of the waiting room and tries to calm me down, he's mechanical and cold, I scream: Where's Carl? he takes hold of me, he holds me tightly, we walk down a hall, we go into an office, some nurses are sitting there, behind the office is a room, we go into that room, Carl

is lying there, the first thing I notice is his eyes, they're black and
blue, violently swollen, two dark arches, his eyes are closed, his lips
are slightly parted, and there's a wheezing sound, it's the respirator
that is wheezing, it's breathing for him. He's alive. He's not going
to make it, they say he's not going to make it, says Martin. I am
sitting there sobbing and holding Carl's hand, and I stroke his
cheek, and say: Little friend, little friend, I love you. I understand
nothing. There's a cloth over his head. I can see his ears. They're
completely intact, so delicate and well formed, as usual, mussels,
marzipan, they sit close to that lovely head. His beautiful ears cause
my despair to grow, which cannot be contained, I have no words
to describe the panic, the pain that makes my body stagger around
the room, this ward, this antechamber, this waiting room to death's
chamber. His beautiful ears show no signs of an accident or death.
A sheet covers his body. Various tubes and drips are attached to him.
I can see the hair on his chest, which, like his ears, lies close to him,
close to his skin, in perfect patterns, reminding me of mussel shells,
of flowers growing in the rainforest, of fern, ready to unfurl. The
respirator breathes in, blows out, Carl's chest fills and empties of
air, Carl's chest rises and falls with calm movements, as if he were
sleeping so sweetly. Why doesn't he have clothes on? I ask. Why is
he naked, why didn't they dress him? What if he's freezing? And I
notice a violent rage, I notice that I don't think they're taking good
care of him, and then Martin says, Martin says:
He was naked when he jumped out of the fifth-floor window.

Roubaud writes:

The scorching   line of light   terror   written in light
stopped   exactly

Where you turn black

Hans Christian Andersen writes in 'The Story of a Mother':

Then they went into Death's great greenhouse, where flowers and trees were strangely intertwined. In one place, delicate hyacinths were kept under glass bells, and around them great hardy peonies flourished. There were water plants too, some thriving where the stalks of others were choked by twisting water snakes, or gnawed away by black crayfish. Tall palm trees grew there, and plane trees, and oaks. There grew parsley and sweet-smelling thyme. Every tree or flower went by the name of one particular person, for each was the life of someone still living in China, in Greenland, or in some other part of the world. There were big trees stunted by the small pots which their roots filled to bursting, and elsewhere grew languid little flowers that came to nothing, for all the care that was lavished upon them, and for all the rich earth and the mossy carpet where they grew. The sad, blind mother bent over the tiniest plants and listened to the beat of their human hearts, and among so many millions she knew her own child's heartbeat. 'This is it,' she cried, groping for a little blue crocus, which had wilted and dropped to one side.

And he writes:

Every human being, you know, has his tree or his flower of life.

We planted a magnolia tree at your gravesite
And we built a wall with a ledge
And on the ledge we placed pots and vases

And we filled the pots and vases with plants
And we filled them with flowers and herbs
And we filled them with trees and bushes
And we planted the forest and spring's growth
In the earth in front of the wall we planted
Ferns, violets, anemone
Lilies of the valley, woodruff
Sweet scented spring forest, green

★

Your older brother got up and spoke at your funeral. He said:

When Carl was young, he was interested in the myths and
fables from Ancient Greece.
The stories absorbed him so much that he wanted to hear
them again and again. Stories about Pegasus, Sisyphus,
Hercules. When his other brothers and cousins got tired of
listening, Carl would ask for one more story, which I was
happy to tell. Carl and I were a lot alike in this way – we
both had a great fascination for history, especially from
antiquity. So, it's ironic that the story of Carl's life ends just
like Aristotle's description of how a tragedy is structured. This
description comes from his work *Poetics*.
You choose a hero, someone you can identify with. A person,
like anyone in the audience, with ordinary character traits and
ordinary minor flaws, but who is one hair nobler, one hair
better. That's how Carl was, to a large degree. I always felt that
he was fairer, more embracing, more open than me. In many
ways, a better person.

We put out a notebook at the dinner after the funeral.

Your twelve-year-old brother wrote:

You have always been my brother. You will always be with
me. Your way. You always turned the worst situation into
something good. Always thinking about others and curious.
All that you were is what gets me through the hard times. You
never got annoyed.

Your twelve-year-old sister wrote:

You are, always have been and always will be the best brother
in the world.

> *All*
> *Always*
> *Never*
>
> *Are*
> *Were*
> *Have been*
> *Will be*

your older brother's daughter is
named
after

you

> *Your way*

Anne Carson's *Nox* includes her translation of poem number 101 by the Roman poet Catullus. He lived around 84–54 BCE. About the translation, Anne Carson writes:

I have never arrived at the translation I would have liked to do of poem 101. But over the years of working at it, I came to think of translating as a room, not exactly an unknown room, where one gropes for a light switch. I guess it never ends. A brother never ends. I prowl him. He does not end.

101)
Many the peoples many the oceans I crossed –
I arrive at these poor, brother, burials
so I could give you the last gift owed to death
and talk (why?) with mute ash.
Now that Fortune tore you from me, you
oh poor (wrongly) brother (wrongly) taken from me,
now still anyway this – what a distant mood of parents
handed down as the sad gift for burials –
accept! soaked with tears of a brother
and into forever, brother, farewell and farewell.

Mallarmé writes:
                    (2
                  feel you
           so strongly – and that you
           are always
           well with

us, father, mother,
<meadows> – but
free, eternal
child, and everywhere
at once –
_____

    and the underside
          – I can

                       (3

say that because
I keep all my
pain for us –
– the pain of
not being – that
you do not know
    – and that I
impose on myself
    (cloistered, further-
more, outside of

                       (4

    life where you
    lead me
        (having opened
   for us a
   world of death)
        _____

            ★

Sitting on the floor surrounded by your handwriting, I find a notebook where you have written:

```
Born of life
Died of life
```

the material substance's strong vibrating and dynamic energy

★

We gathered close together around the coffin, holding each other's hands. You lay there yellow and cold, with your long, blood-encrusted hair, bruised, broken. You had your green jacket on. We placed your guitar beside you, we placed letters and drawings, we placed your great grandfather's wedding ring and my gold ring, we placed a Greenlandic figurine of a man calmly looking out to sea, we placed a blossoming cherry branch, and a coin for the ferryman, we placed a photo of all of us, taken one happy summer day; you're standing in the foreground of the photo, tall and strong, and the image of that photo next to you, now dead, cold and yellow, is one I will never forget. In this trembling moment, life and death in one single image. And we placed oyster shells and beautiful stones and a piece of amber that you found a long time ago. We placed a little bag of pot. From one side of the coffin, your face looked haggard, almost demonic. From the other side, your face looked peaceful and soft, innocent, as when you were a little child, and that's the face we remembered as you. But the other face was there, too. We stood in the chapel, we held each other's hands, and we said goodbye. We said goodbye. We said: 'Safe journey.'

You had your green jacket on

In this trembling moment, life and death are present in one single image

★

77

so intolerably wordless the unbearable
silence that always will be silence always will be your absence
it's not possible to tell your story to describe you in writing you
carried yourself in your living body it was the scent of your skin
your hair the light touching your shoulder cheek the world-light
the sun it was the light of your eyes in twilight your voice your
sleep breath laughter it was your tears lips your graceful neck
your hands resting on your lap everything you carried in your
living body was you your body you no words can describe it
and how I will be able to live with this always

★

Gilgamesh is more than 4,000 years old, the earliest known
surviving work of literature. Gilgamesh was the king of the
city state of Uruk in Mesopotamia – present-day Iraq – at
around 2900 BCE. It is a story about friendship, love, life and
death. Gilgamesh loses his friend, the wild man Enkidu, and
then drags himself, sick with grief, out into the world to beg
Utnapishtim, who's been given eternal life from the gods, to
help him escape death. After enduring many hardships, he
succeeds in finding Utnapishtim, but fails to acquire the gift of
immortality.

Gilgamesh has immense power. The text has travelled through
thousands of years, and it's hard to fathom how it still carries
so much clarity and strength. It's blazed through time like
a literary fireball, full of passion and desperation, bearing
witness to the fact that, as far back as 4,000 years ago, people
considered the pain of loss and death the hardest, most

significant experience in a person's life. Here, Gilgamesh
grieves over Endiku at sunrise, the first day after his death:

O Enkidu, what is this sleep that has seized you,
that has darkened your face and stopped your breath?

But Enkidu did not answer. Gilgamesh
touched his heart, but it did not beat.

Then he veiled Enkidu's face like a bride's.
Like an eagle Gilgamesh circled around him,
he paced in front of him, back and forth,
like a lioness whose cubs are trapped in a pit,
he tore out clumps of his hair, tore off
his magnificent robes as though they were cursed.

And he continues:

the people of Uruk will mourn him, and when
he is gone, I will roam the wilderness
with matted hair, in a lion skin.

When Gilgamesh at last meets Utnapishtim, he says:

I have wandered the world, climbed the most treacherous
mountains, crossed deserts, sailed the vast ocean,
and sweet sleep has rarely softened my face.
I have worn myself out through ceaseless striving,
I have filled my muscles with pain and anguish.
And what in the end have I achieved?

And Utnapishtim answers by telling him the meaning of death:

But man's life *is* short, at any moment
it can be snapped, like a reed in a canebrake.
The handsome young man, the lovely young woman –
in their prime, death comes and drags them away.
Though no one has seen death's face or heard
death's voice, suddenly, savagely, death
destroys us, all of us, old or young.
And yet we build houses, make contracts, brothers
divide their inheritance, conflicts occur –
as though this human life lasted forever.
The river rises, flows over its banks
and carries us all away, like mayflies
floating downstream: they stare at the sun,
then all at once there is nothing.

★

The last text you wrote to me:

```
I'm coming over for dinner on Sunday, big
Madda! I can't wait to see you!
```

That was Wednesday, 11 March 2015, three days before
that gruesome night. The day I flew from New York to
Copenhagen with a little bag containing a few books and
clothes for four days. I landed on Thursday morning. I was
supposed to fly back home on Monday. Monday, 16 March.

Madda: patois for *mother*

80

The respirator breathes in, blows out, Carl's chest fills and empties of air, Carl's chest rises and falls with calm movements, as if he were sleeping so sweetly. Why doesn't he have clothes on? I ask. Why is he naked, why didn't they dress him? What if he's freezing? And I notice a violent rage, I notice that I don't think they're taking good care of him, and then Martin says, Martin says:

He was naked when he jumped out of the fifth-floor window.

I look at Martin, the fear exploding in my head, and ask: What are you saying? Did he try to commit suicide? I can hear that I'm shouting.

No, says Martin. No. He and N took mushrooms. Then he turns away.

I don't understand a thing, I rush out into the waiting room where Carl's friend N is sitting with his face buried in his hands, bent over, and I see N's girlfriend and my sister, and I see my mother and father and my brother-in-law, and my sister embraces me, crying, and I crouch down in front of N, I say: What happened? Tell me everything, tell me the truth, you have to promise me you'll tell the whole truth, you can't leave anything out. And N is ashen, he says: We took some mushrooms late in the afternoon, mushrooms that we bought on the Internet and grew in a closet, and at first I had a bad trip and felt that I couldn't see or hear, I only saw darkness and demons, Carl calmed me down, sat with me, and when it was starting to pass, it hit Carl, but just before the bad trip hit Carl, he was going on about his love for me, saying that he desired me, and that maybe he was a homosexual, and I said: Let's talk about it in the morning, when we're clear in our heads, and then I went and lay down on Joakim's bed, because I was afraid of my own, it's a loft bed, I didn't dare climb up there, and then Carl took a shower, and it was like he was in the shower for several hours, but it probably wasn't several hours, and then, and then, then Carl came walking very quickly and stark naked through the apartment, he walked into his room and lay down on his bed, and then, then I knew something was wrong, because Carl would never walk stark naked through the apartment, and I asked him: Are you okay? And Carl said no, and I went over to him, maybe I shouldn't have, but I went over to him, and he was thrashing around on the bed, pulling at his skin and hair, and grinding his teeth, he was tearing into his skin and his hair as if he couldn't be in his own body, and he said that I didn't understand anything, that there wasn't a day tomorrow, that it was like the end of the world, and he didn't recognize me, his eyes were coal black, and he didn't look like himself, he looked frightening, and I got really scared, and it was like he couldn't see me at all, like he was seeing visions, he saw something I couldn't see, then suddenly he sprang out of bed and began walking back and forth, back and forth, and he was looking over at the window, and I tried to calm him down, I said: Lie down and go to sleep, it'll pass while you're sleeping. But he kept saying that I was trying to foist something on him, that I was selling him false ideas, that I didn't understand anything, then he grabbed me, he grabbed me hard by my arms, and his hands moved up towards my neck, and I was so afraid, I tore myself loose, I ran out the back door in my socks, I didn't dare use the front door, I was worried that he'd follow me, or that it might make him even more crazy. I ran out the back door, and called the police from the backstairs. I said: My friend and I are on mushrooms, I'm afraid that he's going to murder me or jump out the window, you need to get over here right away.

Truth, *(trooth), n. [pl. TRUTHS (troothz, trooths)], [ME. treuthe; AS. treowth, truwth; see TRUE & -TH]. **1.** the quality or state of being true; specifically, a) formerly, loyalty; trustworthiness. b) sincerity; genuineness;*

honesty. c) the quality of being in accordance with experience, facts, or reality; conformity with fact. d) reality, actual existence. e) agreement with a standard, rule, etc.; correctness, accuracy. 2. that which is true; statement, etc. which accords with fact or reality. 3. an established or verified fact, principle, etc.

★

We hold each other's hands, and the mornings are the worst, they're overflowing with anxiety. The first days and weeks, we go from apartment to apartment in Copenhagen, our friends move out to give us their homes to stay in. The anxiety pushes us out of bed each morning, out to face the other bewildered people sitting around the kitchen table, the friends, family, children, youths and adults – we are many, we sleep on air mattresses and sofas, we sleep light, nightmarish sleep or deep, alcohol sleep, and every morning we have to face it all over again. We have to understand. Yet we understand nothing. We're freezing. So we drink coffee. Then we brush our teeth. Then a friend arrives. Our friend says: Now we're going for a walk. Our friend says: Come on. Put one foot in front of the other. We go out. The morning light is sharp. The light drives fear around like oil in water. And we drift. We are drifting lumber, sticks, bits of bone. We are no longer a self. We cannot contain our selves. We are I-less. We have become we.

there is no I anymore, only we

Nothing is real. Language is emptied of meaning.

Shock-language

How 'are' 'you' doing 'now'?
A little 'better'.
Have 'you' had any 'sleep' at all?
Yes, 'I' 'slept' a little.

Quote marks are necessary for describing the new reality, the no-reality, the one we suddenly find ourselves in, a state of emergency, where nothing ordinary resonates or can be established, where nothing in the entire world is recognizable.

The use of quote marks unleashes spontaneous laughter, and the laughter gives brief moments of ease. 'Redemption.'

Should we try to 'eat' now?
Should we 'go' for a walk?

We can only talk with an extreme use of quotation marks; it becomes our code, a way to express the impossible: this state, the unthinkable.

Are 'you' 'okay'?

We use our hands to show this cryptic effacing sign, these constantly fluttering hands around the empty words, which give the empty words some sort of meaning.
'Meaning.'

★

Your older brother got up and spoke at your funeral. He continued:

The tragic element begins when the hero commits *hamartia*, a fatal flaw or a fatal miscalculation. This fatal miscalculation is never malevolent, but is carried out with the best intentions. An action anyone in the audience could commit if the circumstances were in place. A small, insignificant action. When Carl purchased and grew his own hallucinogenic mushrooms, it was not his intention to take his life or do any harm. Carl had taken mushrooms before, with positive effects. Now he wanted to go one step further and grow completely organic ones, to obtain a true and natural high. But the miscalculation in the tragedy is the triggering factor for *peripeteia* – a reversal of fortune. A reversal of fortune is the sudden shift from lucky to unlucky. In the reversal of fortune, you get caught by your good intentions. No doubt, Carl was fortunate; he was always happy and positive, right up until his death. Carl's reversal of fortune occurred when his home-grown organic mushrooms triggered a drug-induced psychosis. During his psychosis, he undressed, opened the window, took a running start and jumped out into the night. A seemingly harmless action started a cascade of events that ended in his death.

Hamartia
Peripeteia

Fortuna, *prop n. [Fortūna] (L.: Fortuna, the name of the Roman goddess representing what is to come, the vicissitudes.)*

Anne Carson writes:

Single motion which departed, leading itself by the hand.

★

85

Tyche, *(Gr.: Τύχη, meaning 'luck')* An ancient Greek term for how a person's fate plays out in life, lucky or unlucky.

This depiction of fate relates to medieval ballads about fortune and misfortune, which can neither be predicted nor averted.

In antiquity, philosophers believed that fate was the expression of an unexpected causal sequence that humans simply could not perceive.

The concept of tyche is personified by Tyche, the goddess of chance. The Romans depicted her identically with Fortuna.

★

I read about psychosis, trying to understand how you can be yourself and not be yourself at the same time. I try to understand how you did not commit suicide, but how your body threw you out of the window from the fifth floor. *You* were not present *in your self* when your body threw you out of the fifth-floor window, you did not know it happened. My brain burns; it cannot get these extreme opposites to fit together; it cannot get this information to form a sequence, *one story*, the story we will have to live with for the rest of our lives, the story about your death, on the one side undeserved and unwanted, and on the other, expressed so violently and resolutely, so absolutely, in a sudden movement that, in a matter of seconds, changed you from being a strong, fortunate young person to a lifeless body on the street in Copenhagen. The psychosis exists between these two states.

> **Psychosis,** *The legal definition: Ruptured/injured/lacking a grasp of reality, loss of reality. An inability to grasp reality.*

In psychiatry, the definition is narrower: the presence of 'productive psychotic phenomena' = hallucinations, delusions, unusual actions as well as signs of 'disintegration' of the mental 'firmness': incoherent speech, unnatural speed of activities (slow or fast).

In scientific diagnostics, the concept of 'psychosis' is avoided. Instead, 'psychotic' is used, since the state cannot be precisely defined.

And I read:

Some mushrooms contain the naturally occurring drug psilocybin, which belongs to the general category of hallucinogens. The drug's effects are similar to LSD. There are also other hallucinogenic plants, but psilocybin mushrooms are the most common.

The mushrooms cause hallucinations, a powerful distortion of sensory input, thinking and feeling. One hears sounds and sees things that aren't there. One loses control over what is happening. The physical experience is altered, and all impressions are distorted, unstable and intrusive. The intoxication is similar to psychosis, and lasts for six to eight hours. With so-called bad trips – a nightmarish state – the high can last much longer. It is often accompanied with nausea and a slight rise in temperature, pulse and blood pressure. The pupils dilate.
There is a great risk for accidents with the use of mushrooms because the user's view of reality is distorted.

Carl: Vegetarian, rarely drank alcohol, liked to smoke a little pot.

Never abused drugs, never addicted, never suicidal.

The dark gaze that your friend N saw. The dilated pupils.
The black swollen eyes that we saw at the hospital and in the
chapel. Caused by the excessive internal bleeding.

The black eyes. Behind them: your beautiful eyes, vanished.

★

We sit in the kitchen of a borrowed
apartment, and time has stopped. We sit around a table in Copenhagen, holding
each other's hands. We can both see and hear the clock that's ticking on the
wall above the refrigerator. But time is broken. It floats, it is floating, all there
is is *now*, it's always only now, nothing more or less than that. We don't know if
it's day or night. We stand outside days and nights now, days and nights have
nothing to do with us; we don't perceive the difference any longer. We have
no hope for the future, we can neither imagine nor sense the future anymore.
We can't see an hour, a quarter of an hour, a minute ahead. We cannot make
plans. We find ourselves in a futureless time. We sit around a kitchen table and
survive, second to second; we rarely get up. We've become rigid, while the
spring light rises and falls in the sky outside: *now that you can no longer be in
chronological time, neither can we.*

Roubaud writes:

in your loss of time I found all of myself included.

Denise Riley writes about the sudden loss of her son, in *Time
Lived, Without Its Flow*:

A sudden death, for the one left behind, does such violence
to the experienced 'flow' of time that it stops, and then
slowly wells up into a large pool. Instead of the old line of

forward time, now something like a globe holds you. You live inside a great circle with no rim. In the past, before J's idiotic disappearance, the future lay in front of me as if I could lean into it gently like a finger of land, a promontory feeling its way into the sea. But now I've no sense of any onward opening but stay lodged in the present, wandering over some vast saucer-like incline of land, like banks of the river Lethe, I suppose, some dreary wide plain. His sudden death has dropped like a guillotine blade to slice right through my old expectation that my days would stream onwards into my coming life. Instead I continue to sense daily life as paper-thin. As it is. But this cut through any usual feeling of chronology leaves a great blankness ahead.

★

We are like children.
Helpless.
Our friends help us with everything.
Our friends come to our rescue.
They gently guide us forward, from one moment to the next.

Those dim and blurry weeks.

★

Much later, we begin to understand:

How your friend N had forgotten his keys when he left your

apartment and called the police. How the police, when they finally arrived, could not get in. How the police rang all the buzzers and there was one person who answered 'Hello' from the front-door intercom.

How your friend N was still intoxicated by the mushrooms. How your friend N mumbled to the emergency call centre that you, under the influence of mushrooms, had said that maybe you were a homosexual. How the message that your friend N feared both for his life and yours was noted in the Independent Police Report as follows:

'A call came in on the radio from central dispatch saying that there was a "fracas" in an apartment on Vesterbrogade, with apparently 2 people present. They indicated that it had something to do with a homosexual relationship, and that a mentally ill person was involved.'

'Dispatch said that the mentally ill person in the apartment had lost control, that the situation was chaotic. A dispatch was put out that it had something to do with a homosexual person. The police did not put the sirens on. The dispatcher did not consider it urgent.'

Consequently, it took the police eight minutes to arrive from the time they received the distress call. The distance between the police station and the address on Vesterbrogade is 500 yards. A distance that takes three minutes by car, at the most, if you don't rush.
The accident happened in a densely populated area of Copenhagen on a Saturday evening. There were lots of patrol cars out on the streets.

So why was it so important for the police that the word homosexual was mentioned? Does this word have anything to do with them not driving over there as though it were an emergency?

So where did they get the term mentally ill from? Do those words have anything to do with the police driving over there without their sirens on?

So were 'homosexual' and 'mentally ill' the reasons why none of the many patrol cars already out was called?

So were 'homosexual' and 'mentally ill' the reasons why you are dead?

> **Homophobia,** (*from* homo- (homosexual) + Gr. -phobia*), irrational fear of, aversion to, or discrimination against homosexuality or homosexuals.*

> **Discrimination,** (*from* L. discriminare 'distinguished between'), *the unjust or prejudicial treatment of different categories of people or things, especially on the grounds of sex, race, ethnicity, age, sexual orientation, as well as physical and psychological handicaps.*

We begin to understand, and what we understand is ghastly.

★

I read the police reports, and I read the autopsy report, and people say that I should not torment myself by reading these reports. But I read manically every testimony, I read about fractures and cause of death, I read about the blood on the street, the blood that runs out of your mouth, I read about your heart that was still beating, I read the interrogation

report, I read the descriptions of your dead mutilated body, both legs broken, several fractures in the pelvis, fractures in the pubic bone on the left side, severe bleeding in the brain, *the underside of the brain is pressed down against the large opening at the skull's base*, the crushed frontal bone, lacerations in the brain's frontal lobes, longitudinal fractures at the top of the skull, and I read the eye-witness accounts about how you 'fell like an animal', how you 'fell like a doll', how you 'came flying from the sky', how you made a 'high-pitched thwack', how the witnesses saw the bones sticking out from your ankle, your hips, your knee. I read all about it and then once again, because I want to understand each and every detail about what has happened to you. I must know what happened to you. Of course I must know what happened to you.
You are my child.

★

The question 'what if?' (N had not left Carl/had remembered his keys when he left the apartment/the police had arrived a few minutes earlier/and were let in by the person who answered the front-door intercom with 'Hello'/and had restrained Carl and brought him to a psychiatric emergency room) is the one path we cannot stop ourselves from going down, and it's the one path we should not go down.

But we must go down the path that's about how N and Carl did not get the help they needed because the words 'homosexual' and 'mentally ill' were in play and dominated the dispatcher's account.

So we file a complaint against the police.
We complain and complain and complain.
And each time we're rejected, we file another complaint.
We get nowhere.

It doesn't surprise us.

Our lawyer writes the final complaint to the Attorney General:

It's hard to imagine a more critical situation than one involving a call from an obviously frightened person saying that there is a threat of both murder and suicide.

The faulty communication in this case shows a culture in the police department of discrimination against homosexuality, which has unfortunately resulted in an important omission in that emergency dispatch call.

There is a significant difference between being mentally ill and being affected by intoxicating drugs, and it is relevant information for the officers who will head out to such a situation. The risk of suicide is significantly greater and more acute if a person is hallucinating, than if someone has been depressed for a long time.

To start with, the two officers were sent out to a 'fracas' and homosexuality. These two pieces of information are all that the officers are told at first, and there is no doubt that the most significant information the officers should have been told was that there was a person under the influence of hallucinogenic drugs, who was in danger of committing suicide.

Our complaint is once more rejected. True, the Attorney General admits that '... **the dispatcher's communication in this case could have been clearer and more precise, and that it would have been appropriate if the police were told immediately that there was a suicidal person when they got the call from Central Dispatch.'**

When Carl jumped from the fifth floor, the police were standing on the street and saw him hit the asphalt. The officers didn't do anything wrong. They simply did not receive accurate information about the seriousness of the situation in time.

THE ANGER IS BLUNT AND BOUNDLESS

★

We walk by the scene of the accident, holding each other's hands. We drag ourselves past the scene of the accident, something drags us towards the scene of the accident. It's a cold day in March when we walk by your building, when we see the spot on the asphalt that you hit when you jumped, when we see the window on the fifth floor that you jumped from. The window is curved and tall, like a cathedral. The window reflects the light, the traffic is loud, and there are people with dogs and bikes everywhere. We're not present in our bodies; we're empty rustling shells. We look up and see the window. We look down and we see the street, the asphalt, we see the little stain on the asphalt, and we steady ourselves on the brick wall and parked cars; we steady ourselves against each other, while our eyes see, while our legs walk. We are all body, bodies that walk, bodies that see; there's no resonance in us, no feelings. We only sense the physical pain: how we are about to fall, crash, how we are lead-heavy, earth-heavy, how there is pain in our arms and legs. And we sense our burning eyes.

Denise Riley writes:

Wandering around in an empty plain, as if an enormous drained landscape lying behind your eyes had turned itself outward. Or you find yourself camped on a threshold between inside and out. The slight contact of your senses with the outer world, and your interior only thinly separated from it, like a membrane resonating on the verge between silence and noise. If it were to tear through, there's so little behind your skin that you would fall out towards the side of sheer exteriority. Far from taking refuge deeply inside yourself, there is no longer any inside, and you have become only outwardness. As a friend, who'd experienced the suicide of the person closest to her, says: 'I was my two eyes set burning in my skull. Behind them there was only vacancy'.

★

Joakim got up to speak at the funeral. Joakim, twenty-four years old. He said:

Carl and I lived side by side since we were kids, right up until the end, when we were sharing an apartment here in Copenhagen. Now, unfortunately, I look back on that place as cursed. It wasn't. It was a fantastic place. And that was only because Carl lived there.

★

The day we packed up your things, emptied your room:

Your older brother collapsed on the street

Your father was at the hospital with an oozing acute sty

I had to go to the dentist because of an acute mycosis in my mouth

Acute

Your laundry

Your duvet

The pillow that had fallen to the floor from the bench under the window

The window

The light that streamed in through the window

★

I sleep with your duvet.
I sleep with your fine light duvet.
I can still smell your skin, your sleep.
I say to myself: You are in your duvet.
I say: You are in your duvet, too.
I say: You are.
I believe, and don't believe, what I say.
I only exist in this moment.
It's the closest I can get to your time.
It's nothing I've decided to do.
It's the only thing that's evident.

★

I wrote in my journal:
9 February 2016.
Sometimes, like last night, I try to access the darkness of his final ten minutes when he was alone in the apartment. What happened? What was he doing? Was he lying in bed, was he standing, was he searching for his friend? What did he see or hear that made him jump? But I can't access it. Naturally, I can't. Or: maybe it's not that obvious. Maybe at some point I'll be able to. And maybe it's crazy to think this way.

Today, I cried on the way to the subway because suddenly I was walking behind the coffin again. Getting up from my chair, hearing all the sounds, jackets rustling, chair legs scraping against the floor, the sweeping sounds of the living, and then – there was the coffin. How we moved forward behind it, how not letting him slip from my sight even for a second felt like both the most impossible and the most important thing in the world. If someone comes between him and me now, I'll kick them down. And I walked furiously away from the coffin when it was lowered into the earth. I flew. I ran away, hating everyone, furious and wild with sorrow. I left all the people and hid in a side street. I didn't cry. I called a taxi. I ordered a taxi and my voice was cold and mechanical.
There is nothing more I can do for him in the whole wide world. I sit in a café in Chelsea. The sky is dark and starless.

I would go to the ends of the earth for you.

But it was not far enough.

★

Gilgamesh wandered desperately in his sorrow across the plains, looking for Utnapishtim, who had survived the flood and therefore received eternal life from the gods. Gilgamesh wants that as well. He is overwhelmed by his fear of death. Along the way, he meets, among others, a proprietress of an inn, and he tells her how he could not bring himself to bury his beloved friend, Enkidu. He cannot accept his death. He will not part from him; he will not part with his body. He says:

For six days I would not let him be buried,
thinking, 'If my grief is violent enough,
perhaps he will come back to life again.'
For six days and seven nights I mourned him,
until a maggot fell out of his nose.
Then I was frightened, I was terrified by death,
and I set out to roam the wilderness.
I cannot bear what happened to my friend –
I cannot bear what happened to Enkidu –
so I roam the wilderness in my grief.
How can my mind have any rest?
My beloved friend has turned into clay –
my beloved Enkidu has turned into clay.

★

In 1865, Walt Whitman wrote the poem 'When Lilacs Last in the Dooryard Bloom'd'. The poem, an elegy, is 206 lines long and divided into 16 sections.

Whitman writes:

98

When lilacs last in the dooryard bloom'd,
And the great star early droop'd in the western sky in the night,
I mourn'd, and yet shall mourn with ever-returning spring.

Ever-returning spring, trinity sure to me you bring,
Lilac blooming perennial and drooping star in the west,
And thought of him I love.

Walt Whitman. In your pocket. Your great grandfather's book.
In the pocket of your green jacket. The strange blessing
when I found it, a strange joy knowing that you were reading
Whitman in the days before your death. That you made it to
reading Whitman. The strange joy, that it was a *sign*.

It's Venus that Whitman is talking about in the poem. Venus,
the morning and evening star. Venus, the goddess of love.
Venus, who hides under a veil of clouds, the ashen light
produced by the planet. Venus, the earth's sister planet.

And *the lilacs, the lilacs*.
The sweet, sweet scent of the white and purple flowers.

> **Elegy,** /ˈɛlədʒi/, *n. (from Fr. elegie; L. elegīa; Greek ἐλεγεία literary
> poem in elegiacs, in Hellenistic Greek also elegiac poetry as a genre
> < ἔλεγος sung lament). 1. a. A song or poem of lamentation, esp. for the
> dead; a memorial poem. Also as a mass noun. b. In Greek and Latin
> poetry: a poem written in elegiac metre (hence) a poem in another
> language based on or influenced by this.*

★

I'm crouching in front of N and then Martin says: We need to go see the doctor now, we need to go see the doctor, and he and I go into the doctor's office, which is just across the hall from where Carl is, and I'm crying, and we sit down, and the doctor says: Yes, it's a very sad affair, but no matter where Carl is now, he regrets what he's done. And I become furious and say: He is nowhere, and he regrets nothing whatsoever. And then the doctor says: We should talk about whether you'll donate any of Carl's organs, because he's not going to make it, there's no way, the only reason we're keeping him artificially alive is in case you're interested in donating some of his organs. And Martin and I look at each other with wild eyes, and we say: Yes, yes, we would like to, that's what Carl would've wished. And everything starts sinking, and I say: What do you mean that he's not coming back? How can you know for sure? And the doctor says: The damage is too massive, there's no hope, he sustained so many fractures from the fall, such massive brain damage, survival is not possible. Survival is not possible. It's a small, stuffy office, and we say: Yes, yes, we would like to donate some of his organs, that is what he would've wished, and still we understand nothing. We go back to the waiting room and I say to Martin: I can't bear that our children will now live with this trauma for the rest of their lives. And my father says: We should call them in Brooklyn. And I say: Can you do it? I can't. And then he calls, it's early in the evening in Brooklyn now, and my youngest sons are with my husband, my father calls, he says: Something terrible has happened, it's Carl, there is not much left of him. I can't listen anymore, my brain burns, I can't bear that they have to know what has happened, that my children have to hear this gruesome news, this insane, gruesome news, and I take the phone, and I can hear my husband's voice, and I say: It's Carl, it's true, you should come as soon as possible, you should come now, and I can hardly speak. We sit in the waiting room all night, and we go in to see Carl, and we hold his hands, *and we kiss him, and I say: Little friend, little beloved friend, Carlo, Carlito, and it wheezes, wheezes, the respirator wheezes and clicks, he looks like himself, and he does not look like himself, the coal-black, swollen eyes, his forehead covered with a cloth so we won't see his broken head, and we say: What have you done? What have you gone and done to yourself?*

*

The demonic was with you as you were lying in the coffin. One side of your face: demonic. We could not stop thinking that the demons you saw during your psychotic episode had left a mark on you. We could not stop fearing that these demons had overtaken you, overtaken *your soul*. Eradicated that which we knew as *you*. These demented thoughts. This insane fear. The madness streamed through us, and we felt powerless, ignorant, small, exactly as the people of ancient Greece felt, who attributed to Fortuna everything that was incomprehensible, gruesome, completely meaningless.

And grief.

Like Cicero's grief, when he mourned the loss of his daughter Tullia. She died in February 45 BCE, one month after she gave birth to her second child. Cicero isolated himself for months in his villa near Astura, *broken by sorrow*. The loss hit him harder than anything in his life. But it also set in motion his literary production. As early as the spring of 45 BCE, he began writing a *consolatio*, solace writing, which has been lost, unfortunately. And he wrote *Hortensius*, a fragmented revival or exhortation manuscript, a common genre at that time, with the purpose of turning readers around to philosophy as the path to a fulfilling human existence. He threw himself into philosophy as a cure for pain. His literary focus completely changed direction.

There is *before*.
And *after*.

Between these two poles:

That which changes everything forever.

I am someone else.

I am forced to be someone else.

Nothing is familiar.

Nothing.

This is exactly what Nick Cave says in the documentary *One More Time With Feeling* (2016). He lost his fifteen-year-old son the same way I lost my son. Nick Cave's son jumped or fell from a cliff after he had taken hallucinogenic drugs with his friend. Nick Cave says in the film:

Most of us don't want to change, really. I mean, why should we? What we do want is a sort of a modification of the original model. We keep on being ourselves, but just hopefully better versions of ourselves.
But what happens when an event occurs that is so catastrophic that you just change?

You change from a known person to an unknown person.
So then, when you look at yourself in the mirror, you
recognize the person that you were, but the person inside the
skin is a different person.

★

Sixth dream (3 May 2016)
I'm sitting under an overhang in the shade with lots of
booksellers. There's a street, and on the other side of the
street is a bench. On the bench sits Carl's friend, N. The sun
is shining; we're surrounded by green trees. I understand that
Carl is in prison for stealing books. Several booksellers talk on
phones. They're talking to lawyers and police to find out how
harsh his punishment should be. They tell me that he's going
to get a very harsh punishment. Then Carl walks up and sits
down on the bench next to his friend N. I shout: Carl! I shout:
Come over here! He looks shyly or shamefully down at the
ground. His hair is shaved, and he has tattoos of buildings all
around his head. Come here! I shout again. Mum! I shout, I
shout: MUM. Then he gets up and changes into a little white
goat. The goat crosses the street and comes over to me, and I
scratch it behind its ears and stroke its fur. Then the goat says:
AH. Then it says: MUM. Then it turns back into Carl, and
I embrace him. Look, he says, I have the Manhattan skyline
around my head. He does. Good that you're not dead, I say.
I'm getting a very harsh punishment, he says. I'm afraid that
he will be beaten up and abused in prison. Carl goes back to
his friend N. I know that I can't cross the street. I know that
I'm not going to see him for a long time.

Seventh dream (16 May 2016)
Carl is locked in a freezing dark cellar. A young man has locked him in there. We learn that Carl will never be able to come up into the light again.

Books. Transformation. Punishment.
Crossroads. Imprisonment.
Dark. Never.

★

> **Pan,** *(Gr., etym. uncertain), Grecian god of shepherds, identified by the Romans as Faunas. Pan, whose cult was originally located in Arcadia, in contrast to the anthropomorphic (humanlike) Greek gods, is usually represented with horns, beard, tail and goat legs. Along with the nymphs, he could be found in fields and forests, and those who met him would suffer from a 'panic attack'.*
>
> *Fear of nature and nature within oneself, desolate places, the dark forest, and, first and foremost, that 'groundless' anxiety we call 'panic' was named after Pan.*
>
> *Pan is often associated with mischievousness that is neither benign nor malicious. It is as if Pan creates misfortune for the sake of entertainment.*
>
> *Pan is the only Greek deity who dies.*

★

A month after the funeral, we return home to Brooklyn. The days pass, and the days are empty, but filled with shock and grief. I sit near the window and stare at the sky, the clouds. I sit at the table and stare out into space. I have no

needs. I have no desire. I force myself to eat. I force myself
to sleep. In the evening, I drink wine so that I can fall asleep.
I drink myself drunk. I collapse into sleep. I buy nothing.
I'm indifferent to my appearance, my clothes, my impact on
others. I avoid people I don't know really well. I don't dare
to be alone. When I'm alone, there's nothing that keeps me
from going insane. No boundaries. I can't control myself.
I have no means of controlling myself. Nothing works. No
routines work when I'm alone. I have no routines. To any
work-related offers, I immediately say no. I consistently say
no. I'm indifferent. I have no ambition. In the afternoon, I lie
on the sofa. I watch TV series. One season after another. I lie
on the sofa until evening. This is the only thing that soothes
me, because it makes me disappear. Like being drunk. It's a
sedative. I don't say much. I only get involved if it's absolutely
necessary: I simply maintain what it takes to stay alive. I can
hardly manage to take care of my children. I try. I prioritize
time with my children and my husband over everything else. It
happens by itself, it's instinctive. I am deeply dependent on my
husband and my friends. Once in a while, I manage to write to
my friends. They write to me. Their letters keep me alive. Love
keeps me alive. My children keep me alive. Just barely alive.

Roubaud writes:

I rarely go out as if locking myself in the minimal space could
make you real again because you lived here with me.

                              you are real

                              I am here

Your older brother got up and spoke at the funeral. He
continued:

Aristotle believed that tragedy after a reversal of fate would
inspire fear and compassion in the audience. Compassion, for
those who do not deserve trouble. Fear, when someone gets
into trouble who, in many ways, is like ourselves. Our equal.
The impact on the audience needs to be strong and gripping.
The audience has to experience catharsis – a shock-like effect
that makes the audience's hair stand on end. And here is the
crux of the tragedy and this entire unfortunate situation. We
have compassion for Carl – and we feel fear that we ourselves
under certain circumstances could have met the same fate.
After the tragedy, the audience will leave the theatre feeling
humble about their own ability to avoid trouble, and will
think twice about looking down on one of their fellow human
beings, whose life has ended in a failed situation. I hope
that everyone with us today in this room will learn from this
tragedy.

★

*We sit in the waiting room all night, and we go in to see Carl,
and we hold his hands, and we kiss him, and I say: Little friend,
little beloved friend, Carlo, Carlito, and it wheezes, wheezes, the
respirator wheezes and clicks, he looks like himself, and he does not
look like himself, the coal-black, swollen eyes, his forehead covered*

*with a cloth so we won't see his broken head, and we say: What
have you done? What have you gone and done to yourself? I lift the
sheet off his body and see that a broken bone is sticking out of his
ankle. And I say to the nurse: He has asthma, maybe that's why
he can't breathe, maybe he has difficulty breathing, you should
give him some asthma medicine. And she takes my hand and says:
Then we'll give him some Ventolin, don't you think you should go
home and get a little rest? On a cart there is a little bag with a thin
woven bracelet, it's Carl's, the only thing he had on when he was
brought in, it was cut off his wrist, and I think: He was born in
this hospital, and when the nurse came and put him in my arms,
he had a bracelet on, a bracelet that said who he was, our child, a
boy, born at 2:32 p.m. I think: You came into the world here, and
you will die here, a bracelet is fastened to you, a bracelet is cut off,
I take the little bag and put it in my pocket, I squeeze the bag in
my pocket, I go back to the waiting room, and it's light outside,
it's nearly six o'clock on Sunday morning, and then we go home.
My sister and I go home. Martin goes home. I lie fully dressed on
my sister's sofa and sleep for an hour, wake at seven o'clock to the
sound of my sister's shrieking, she's lying in bed screaming and
crying, and we can't figure out what to do, we're just staggering
around the apartment, and my sister wakes up her ten-year-old son
who's been deep in his sweet unsuspecting sleep, and, crying, she
tells him what happened, and he cries, understanding nothing, his
face is pale and transformed, the shock on a face, on his, the way
shock destroys a face, and my sister and I take a taxi back to the
hospital, and we sit with Carl, we sit with Carl, and Martin comes,
and his wife and their twelve-year-old daughter Malu, Carl's sister,
come, Carl's friend N and his girlfriend come, my parents come,
Martin's father, my oldest son comes, and he wails, he stands next
to Carl wailing, he falls to the floor, screaming and crying, and
we tell them all what happened, more people come, many people*

*come, family, friends, Carl's friends, Carl's two ex-girlfriends come,
the waiting room is filled with people, some go to get fruit, some
get coffee, we sit with Carl and wait and wait for the doctors to
declare him brain-dead, so he can be brought down and operated
on to remove his organs, so they can turn off the respirator, so he
can die. A doctor shows us how many fractures he has in his body,
we all stand in the corridor, he shows us an X-ray, we have two
doctors in the family who understand what they see, they're shocked,
they've never seen so many fractures in a body, in a head, they tell
us that, and we stand in the corridor, and the doctor tells us what
he's discovered, and I look at the images, Carl's bones, Carl's skull,
I don't understand anything, but I understand that Carl will die,
I begin to understand that Carl will die, and the day passes, more
people come, we're a very large group, we fill the entire waiting
room, we have moved into the waiting room of the neuro intensive-
care unit, and the doctor asks Martin and me what we will donate,
he says that the kidneys are sound, the pancreas, that one of his
lungs can be used, the other is torn. He says: Will you donate his
heart? He has a strong young heart, you can think it over, he
says, and I cry and cry, his heart, his heart, and we go back to the
waiting room, and we sit with Carl, the day passes, the hours, the
minutes, the seconds, and then towards the evening many start to
leave, and at last it's just me and my sister waiting, we are waiting
for her oldest son Joakim, for Carl's cousin Joakim, who's grown up
with Carl, as if they were brothers, who lives with Carl and N, for
him to come home from Spain, he is in Spain, he could not catch
an earlier flight, we are waiting for Joakim, and at last he comes,
ten o'clock in the evening he arrives, N is with him, and Joakim
sits there stiff and pale in a chair and does not dare to go in to see
Carl, but at last he goes, he goes in to Carl, and we sit in the waiting
room, and then we go home, and my brother-in-law gives us each a
glass of wine, and we fall over, and I sleep on the sofa in my clothes,*

I don't understand how I can sleep, but my body falls asleep, and now my husband and two youngest sons in Brooklyn are on their way, they're sitting on the plane, and I sleep, I sleep five hours, then I wake up because my whole body is shaking violently, it's nearly six o'clock, it's Monday morning, Monday, 16 March 2015, and I think: I cannot give his heart away, I cannot bury him without his heart, we cannot make him heartless.

★

We're sitting on the floor, holding each other's hands. We're writing on the back of an envelope. We write:

WHAT INJURIES?
WHAT EXAMINATIONS?
WHY IS HE HOOKED UP TO A RESPIRATOR –
IS IT ONLY BECAUSE OF THE DONOR
TRANSPLANT?

WE WANT TO TALK

BROKEN BACK OR NECK?
ARE HIS ORGANS 'CRUSHED'?
THE BRAIN
FUNCTIONING
KIDNEYS

LIVER

WHEN

We're sitting together around a table in a kitchen with a female undertaker. There are many of us, maybe twenty, maybe thirty, and now apparently the undertaker is here, and once in a while a baby screams, and, once in a while, laughs with excitement, while the undertaker tries to explain what we need to consider; she tries to explain what's going to happen. We can't understand. We write down notes on a piece of paper. We write:

SEE HIM?
    CHAPEL?
WHAT CLOTHES WILL HE WEAR? (COLLECT THEM, WHO?)
XL COFFIN, HE'S TOO TALL
DISCOUNT?

WHERE? (CEMETERY)

And the baby laughs. The baby throws a ball up in the air and laughs.

★

Denise Riley writes:

I never abandoned him in his life, and I've no intention of starting now, 'just because he's dead'. What kind of a reason would that be? I tried always to be there for him, solidly. And I shall continue to be. (The logic of this conviction: in order to be there, I too have died.)

A vicarious death. If a sheet of blackness fell on him, it has fallen on me too. As if I also know that blankness after his loss of consciousness.

This state is physically raw, and has nothing whatever to do with thinking sad thoughts or with 'mourning'. It thuds into you. Inexorable carnal knowledge.

★

I wrote in my journal:

27 January 2016.

I can't remember the last time I saw Carl. Was it last year, on 24 January? Was it in February? Was I also in Denmark last February? I think so. But I can't manage to read the emails we wrote to each other to find out. The sun beats down and melts the snow. This morning I received two photos from the stonemason of the plaque. It'll be put up tomorrow. The butterfly is beautiful. There's space on the wall for many more plaques – my own, for instance. I sat down and cried. To see his name in glittering gold on the cold marble plaque that looks like skin. Grey skin with black veins. Dead skin. To see his name. And the dates, the numbers of the years, the first, which is wonderful, and the last, so terrible that words can't reach it. I'm about to burst from rage and despair. Feelings are no help. This plaque seals the grave. Now, he's part of eternity.

★

Butterfly, gold on marble skin, Mnemosyne.
Mnemosyne, found all over Europe, but was also a Greek goddess.
Goddess of memory, and the Muses' mother, but also a river.
The river of forgetfulness in Hades is Lethe, drink from it, you forget everything.
Everything you have suffered and learned in life on earth vanishes.
Vanishes, and then you wander around senselessly before rebirth.
The rebirth that is avoided when you drink from Mnemosyne.
Mnemosyne gives you omniscience, insight into everything.
Everything you will remember, understand, from your life, and then you can rest.
Rest and enjoy Elysium's green fields of eternity.

we gave you a coin for the ferryman

                                        we don't believe in anything

and yet we gave you the coin

                                        you live in your name

★

I should have told you about the fine little gold plaque from 300–200 BCE, found in 1969 in the ancient city of Hipponion, near Monteleone di Calabria, now called Vibo Valentia. I should have told you about Orpheus' mystery cult and other cults that promised a happy afterlife for the initiated. I should have told you that Orpheus was the son of Calliope, muse of song and poetry. I should have told you that he invented the lyre. I should have told you that the little gold plaque might have a connection to the mystery cult. I should have told you about the inscription on the gold plaque. I should have taken you with me to the Museo Archeologico Statale Vito Capialbi so you could've seen it with your own eyes. You should have imbibed its message. You should have read:

This is Mnemosyne's work. When you are about to go off

to Hades' well-built home, there's a spring to the right,

by which stands a white cypress.

There the dead souls go to refresh themselves.

Don't go near that spring!

Beyond it you'll find fresh water flowing in

from Mnemosyne's pool. The guardians stand over it.

With their penetrating minds, they will ask

What are you seeking in Hades' murky shade?

Say: 'I am a child of the earth and star-studded sky.

I am parched with thirst and about to perish, so give me swiftly

fresh water to drink from Mnemosyne's pool.'

And indeed they will speak with

the Queen of the Underworld,

and they will give you water to drink from Mnemosyne's pool.

And after, you will go on the sacred way where all the other

initiates and famed bacchants wander.

I pray that you've found Mnemosyne's clear water so that
you may be freed from having to return to this world, this
wheel that people are forced to run around on, this noisy
stage, this aimless place of desire and greed, meaninglessness
and repression, violence, and the endless repetition of folly
and stupidity, naivety and gruesomeness. Generation after

generation. May you not be reborn, may you not have to start over with empty shining eyes, learning everything all over, only to die again.

and still I don't believe in anything

Inger Christensen writes:

Is this flickering of wings only a shoal
of light particles, a quirk of perception?
Is it the dreamed summer hour of my childhood
shattered as by lightning lost in time?

No, this is the angel of light, who can paint
himself as dark mnenosyne Apollo,
as copper, hawk moth, tiger swallowtail.

★

Roubaud writes:

Your name's an irreducible trace. There is no possible
negation of your name.

whenever I see or think your name, you exist.

And Roubaud writes:

When your death is done. and it will be done because it speaks. when your death is done. and it will be done. like any death. like anything.

When your death is done. I shall be dead.

Always is done, when the ones you love die.
As long as they live, you are loved.
As long as you are loved, you exist.

Community in death.
We are alone in our bodies.

★

Most of what I read about raw grief and lamentation is fragmentary. It's chaotic, not artistic. Often, the writer doesn't have the strength to use capital letters after full stops. Often, the writer doesn't have the strength to complete the fragment. It *can't* be completed. The writing stays open and pours this inability out through everything that can't be expressed. A hole in which death vibrates. It's not possible to write artistically about raw grief. No form fits. To write about *actual* nothingness, the absence of life. How? To write about the silent unknown that we are all going to meet – how? If you want to avoid sentimentality, the pain stops the sentence mid-sentence. Words sit inadequate and silly on the lines, the lines stop abruptly on their own. The language that's always followed me and been my life, can't do anything. The language gasps, falls to the ground, flat and useless. Language's mourning clothes are ugly and stinky.

To comprehend the incomprehensible is not linguistic. This recognition is a wounded animal, the living wounded flesh that does not understand why it fell and can't get up, and it's a distant hollow whistling in a deep darkness, which you can't decode. I stick with death, because nothing else is possible. I stick with death, because it's my child's reality. He is in that reality – death is the reality. Those are the conditions. I have to accept that I will never see him again, and I have to accept that I must live with that acknowledgement so that it doesn't kill me. The unfinished and imperfect is the nature of grief. The leaps, unpredictable. The poet, who lies there like a wounded animal listening to the distant hollow whistling. The poet, whose language turns ugly and stinky in an unflattering way. The poet, who cannot get up by means of her writing, her language, who hates her writing, her language, hates and detests it. The poet, who, within a second, realizes that writing and language mean nothing in the face of death. In the face of the absolute, nothing gives meaning. That shock. That veil that's pulled away from your eyes: what once meant everything, means nothing.

Nothing. Means.

Roubaud writes:

I face words with discontent

For a long time I couldn't go near them

Now, I hear, and spew them out.

And he writes:

I could not speak for nearly thirty months.

★

I look for you and I do not find you.
Never.
It's not possible.
You are gone.
All the conceptions are pure desperation, delusion and
masquerade.
To understand, I need to sink myself down into the silence,
the nothingness.
The dense darkness.
Remain there, lingering, so that it penetrates all my cells.
So I can carry it with me.

Mallarmé writes:

> no – I will not
> give up
>   nothingness
>
>   ———
>
>   father — — — I
> feel nothingness
>   invade me

Roubaud writes about the dead beloved:

You move, you breathe.

But the silence is absolute.

★

It's nearly six o'clock, Monday morning, Monday, 16 March 2015, and I think: I cannot give his heart away, I cannot bury him without his heart, we cannot make him heartless. I'm crying, the most lonely, inarticulate kind of crying, when I force myself to take a shower. I step into the shower cubicle, stand in the shower thinking about his last, gruesome shower, the shower he took while he was having a psychotic episode, that shower he came out of naked and delusional, that shower leading to his final action. I can't take a shower, I will never take a shower again, the water feels like needles against my skin, shards of broken glass, torture. I look at myself in the mirror, look at my breasts, look at my stomach, I see the scar from the caesarean, and I beat my breasts, my stomach, beating uncontrollably, this useless body, which will always be marked by his birth, I hate my body with intensity, and I want it dead, I want to find its vanishing point, I can't stop hitting myself, and I'm roaring, my sister comes in and says: Put your clothes on, we're going. She looks at me with wild eyes, she says: Come on, do it, laying her hand on my shoulder, and I do it, I do as I'm told, mechanically, I put on clean clothes, I go into the kitchen, I drink coffee, I smoke, we can't stop shaking, we call a taxi, my sister and I go down the stairs of the building where all of our children have grown up, where I once lived above her, and the sight of the stairs makes me sick, Carl ran here

once, happy, little, big, a graduate, with his brothers and cousins, this
building, the closest I have to a home in Denmark, this place, the
longest he lived anywhere in his life, we go down the stairs, we get in
the car, we see nothing, everything is flickering, and seems to belong
to another world, we do not want to see it, we hold each other's
hands, arrive, take the lift up to the tenth floor, and we go in to see
Carl, who looks worse than yesterday, more yellow, more waxy, the
nurse says he hasn't had any reflexes during the night, I touch his
arm, his hand, his cheek, I look at his mouth, half open with those
familiar teeth, the soft lips, a mouth looking like at any moment
it'll smile, speak, it's unbearable to be next to him, crying, we walk
into the waiting room. And the nurse's tenderness, her warmth,
she gives us dignified care the entire time, she gets us through the
hours like a goddess, the hours, the hours, and then my husband
and my two youngest sons are suddenly standing there before us,
brought from the airport by my husband's brother, their faces look
exceedingly old, my twelve-year-old son looks exceedingly old, his
body is having difficulty standing upright, and we hug each other
hard, and they go in to see Carl, but Johan cannot, Johan sits on
a chair, paralyzed, silent, no expression, I cannot reach him, he has
disappeared, his face is a grey mask, he's turned to stone, the others
go in to see Carl, and we look at each other with wide, panicked
eyes, and death is in our eyes, the horror, we cannot make contact,
we sit in the waiting room, and after a while people begin to arrive,
filling the waiting room, there aren't enough chairs, we are thirty
people, we are forty people, I don't know how many people we are,
and the whole time some go in to see Carl, and the whole time some
come out, looking more dissolved, grey, like strangers, lifeless. As if
death creeps into their faces, marks and ages them, sometimes I can't
recognize them, my friends, my family, I look at their faces, and they
turn into a flickering in the greyness, this is how grief materializes,
this is how grief looks. Martin and I say to the doctor that we will

donate his kidneys and pancreas and the lung that works, and we say: We will not donate his heart. We sign some papers, we stand out in the hall with the doctor, we understand nothing. Then a trauma psychologist enters the waiting room, he says that everyone who is not Carl's parents and siblings should leave, but Martin says no, everyone should stay, these are Carl's people, and the trauma psychologist doesn't know what he should do, but then he says, fine, if that's what you want, and he then talks to us about what we can expect to experience now, how everything will feel unreal for a very long time, how we won't be able to do very much, and that's okay, it's just the way it is, and then he suggests that we describe how we got the message about the accident and how we're related to Carl, and we do that, it takes a long time, he says that we shouldn't 'seek treatment' for at least six months. The brain needs permission to process first, the human brain is able to come far by itself, he says, but N, who's already visited the psychiatric emergency room, needs treatment, he says, because he witnessed the accident, he saw and heard the fall, he'll need help, but everyone else, he says, you will be haunted by flashbacks, and that's all right, it's completely normal, it's the way the brain gets used to what's happened, and the trauma psychologist leaves, and we stare at each other with our terrified eyes, and then the doctor comes and says, it's not long until Carl will be declared brain-dead and so it's time to say goodbye, he says, if you want to go in and say goodbye to Carl, do it now, who'll go in first? And no one gets up, no one can manage that goodbye, but then my youngest son gets up, Zakarias, twelve years old, he gets up and says he will. And he looks at Johan and says: Come on. And Johan, who has not yet gone in to see Carl, gets up reluctantly, he couldn't manage it, he could not, but now he gets up, and the two of them go to see Carl, holding each other close, they walk the short distance down the hall and go into Carl's room, and it is the longest distance ever, the most preposterous walk, and only two or three of

us are allowed to be in the room at a time, and then it's my turn,
I cry and cry, Johan and Zakarias are sitting next to him, still
and completely silent, they've put on Bob Marley's 'Redemption
Song' and it's playing on a loop, Carl loved that song, it was the
last song on Marley's last album, the last album he recorded before
he died of cancer, 'won't you help to sing / these songs of freedom /
cause all I ever had / redemption songs.' It's just Marley's voice and
Marley's guitar, like a psalm, my sons with bowed heads, I look at
Carl diminishing, his disappearing body, his missing consciousness,
he looks almost like a corpse now, but the respirator still wheezes,
pulling air into him, blowing it out, the chest heaves and lowers
mechanically, it's unbearable, I hold his hand, but I can't manage
it, I run out, I run down the hall and fall into the arms of the first
person I meet, I am dizzy, and I sob in the person's embrace, what
should we do, what should we do, there's nothing we can do, but we
still have to wait.

★

When your younger brother turned thirteen, he wrote many
poems about your death. In his last poem, he wrote:

To thank the birds for chirping

the trees for blooming.

To grow with the trees

to sing with the birds.

I am resilient as roots.

I am strong as wind.

You taught me to live

when you were still here.

Now you are here

to guide me

watching me through

my own eyes.

We are in each other

★

My first book, a poetry collection, was published in 1991. I wrote it when you were a baby. I wrote it as I nursed you, as I rocked you, as I got to know you, as you learned to crawl and walk. There's a poem in the book in which I describe a dream I had when you were a year old. A dream about you. In this poem:

I woke
and the dream will not leave me
my son is about to drown
and I can't save him
his brand-new self
soft as a bear's snout
sinks in the clear water

Here was my anxiety over losing you. Here was the powerlessness – not being able to save you from death. An anxiety so overwhelming. The worst that could happen: that you'd vanish.

When you were sixteen years old, I wrote two poems about
death:

When death takes something from you
give it back
give back what you got
from the dead one
when he was alive
when he was your heart
give it back to a rose,
a continent, a winter day,
a boy regarding you
from the darkness of his hood

When death takes something from you
give it back
give back what you got
from the dead one
when you stood in the rain in the snow
in the sun and he was alive
and turned his face towards you
as if wanting to ask something
you no longer remember and he
has also forgotten and it's
an eternity
an eternity ago now

You are the one hiding in the hood's darkness. I thought
intensely about you as I wrote those two poems. I *saw* you
before me as I wrote them. I didn't know why, I didn't ask
myself why, the poems came to me as something from you,
something I could not understand. All I understood was that I

obviously had written two poems about death, and that you in a way *gave* me the images – or that something associated with your *being* got me to write them. The sun, the rain, the snow. Your face turning questioningly towards mine.

I read the two poems out loud at your funeral. I realized that, as early as when you were a year old, I'd received a sign in my dream that you would vanish from me. As early as when you were sixteen years old, I saw you hiding in death's dark hood. That I had already predicted the eternity that would replace your life, the eternity I now live with, and which you are absorbed by. Just as I dreamed that you fell and hurt yourself shortly before you fell to your death from the fifth floor.

But images and signs cannot be interpreted before they're played out in concrete events. You only understand them in retrospect. That's why omens can only be expressed. As language, as poetry. It becomes an experience that belongs to the future, which can *express*, though they are not yet experienced in *reality*. That's what poetry does sometimes. And it's one of its most beautiful qualities. It's also what makes poetry dangerous and portentous. The feeling of knowing something that you can't understand yet or connect to anything in reality. As if poetry makes it possible to move freely in time, as if linear time is suspended while you write and a corner of the future becomes visible in a brief and mystical moment.

But poems also say something about giving back what the dead gave us when they were alive. That the dead's being, in a way, still needs a place in life, and we should pass on the love they gave us. Here lies the hope. A hope that what you gave me will grow in others, if I am able to share it. And that my love is strengthened and made more beautiful because now it contains your love. This must not be destroyed by sorrow. It says in the poem, 'give it back'. As if giving goes back and forth all the time. From the living to the living. From the dead to the living. And from the living to the dead. A circular movement, not linear.

Even still, these poems fill me with rage and a violent hatred for the predictions they contain. It's an impotent rage. A rage that reminds me of what I experienced as a child. Just as children do not understand the forces they're up against (the adults and their incomprehensible actions and refusals), the bereaved do not understand death. But there's nothing to do about it. You can rage as much as you want, nothing will ever come of it. The adults decide and death decides. You can't escape the loss of love, from the adults, from the dead. Hard and furious and despairing, children and the bereaved must struggle on through life, and hope that the love underlying the feeling of loss is larger than the loss itself, and that this love creates love and compassion.

A heart, a rose, a winter day. A boy who drowns in the clear water.

The world's beauty and cruelty. Love's power.

★

Joakim got up and spoke at the funeral. He continued:

Carl had many great thoughts and ideas, but his greatest passion was for community. Since his death, I've been living with our little grieving group. The grieving group is together every single day; we live together, eat together, drink and smoke together. What's completely absurd about the grieving group is that Carl's own death had to happen to create this community he so ardently wished for. Family and friends have become melded together into a single organism, which Carl would be insanely happy to experience. He won't get to. But we live on with his spirit, because he's brought us together at this difficult time. And we should never lose track of this. Life is too short.

> *The grieving group*: everyone who loved you, who loves you.
> And those who love us.

★

We wish people still wore mourning armbands the first year.

We wish people still wore black the first year.

We wish our mark could be visible so that others could see our mark.

We wish rituals still existed.

So we make our own rituals.

Our friends make rituals.

So our friends eat with us every evening.

So our friends call us every morning.

So our friends take care of our children.

So our friends sit with us the whole day, while nothing happens.

So our friends keep us alive, while nothing happens.

Only the burning pain happens.

In the stopped time, burning pain.

Our friends carefully wash the bloody wound.

They ritually wash it every day

Our invisible stigma.

> *The community as something just as absolute as death.*
>
> *The community as the only possibility.*

★

Later, I learn to be alone. Later, I want to be alone. When I'm alone, I watch TV series all day. Or I wander aimlessly around the city, the park, around and around, nothing I see makes an impression on me, nothing I see gladdens me. I see a tree, a person, I confirm: a tree, a person. Nothing penetrates, nothing leaves an impression on me, nothing interests me. My doctor says I need to make an appointment with her. I don't. She calls again, repeating that I need to make an appointment. So I do. When I walk in the door, she says: *You know, the worst thing a person can experience is losing a child.* I start to laugh. She tells me to drink less, but don't stop now. If you want, she says, I can give you pills to take instead. I tell her that I don't want her pills. I say that I'm completely indifferent to my drinking. My doctor says: You should make an appointment with a grief counsellor. I don't. She calls again, repeating that I need to make an appointment with a grief counsellor. So I take the subway over to the grief counsellor. Three times, I take the subway over to the grief counsellor. It makes no difference. She asks me to fill out a questionnaire. She reads my answers and says that I don't suffer from 'complicated grief'. She says: Your grief is normal. The questionnaire seems very American to me.

Later, I begin to box. Three times a week, I go boxing. I hit hard, and I kick hard. I refine my technique. I become better at boxing than I've ever been before. My body becomes strong. A strong sheath around the unknown terrifying uncertainty that is now me.

Denise Riley writes:

It's not the same 'I' who lives in her altered sense of no-time, but a reshaped person. And I don't know how she'll turn out. If writing had once been a modest work of shaping and correcting, now all your small mastery has been smashed by the fact of your child's death.

★

I wrote in my journal:
28 February 2016.
The first real spring day. I recognize the sharp light as something brutal, raw and unmerciful. When we dragged ourselves around the streets in the days after your death, with the slowness of old men, walking feebly, cursing spring, hating it with every fibre in our bodies, it was nauseating and

intolerable to see all the young happy people. We bit our lips until they bled. Our jaws were hard as stone from rage and horror.

I think of you with enormous love. Soon I'll begin to write a book.

Yesterday, your father wrote to me. He wrote: *I am in complete darkness.*

Mallarmé writes:

>   no more life for
>
>   —
>
>   me
>   and I feel
>   I am lying in the grave
>   beside you.

*

I wrote in my journal:
1 March 2016.
Now, it's March. The first day of the month you vanished.

On 7 December 2010, you wrote to me:

Dear Mum, Why don't we Skype or talk in some other way?
I miss you so much and cannot wait until the eighteenth.

The 18 December *arrived* and you travelled to see us. You were only eighteen when we moved to Brooklyn with your two younger brothers. You didn't want to come. You had just graduated from high school, you wanted to go off and travel, you wanted to make it on your own. You were proud, *grown up*.

So often I've regretted that we didn't insist on you coming with us. Later, you came and lived with us for nearly two years. *That precious time.* The time we had together. The time you had. *Your life.*

How one learns to put a value on what's lamented: the all-too-short life.

Every visit, when you reluctantly faced returning to Denmark, you'd cry all the way to the airport.

The last time you travelled home, a few days after New Year's in 2015, you told me that you had learned how to deal with saying goodbye. You no longer cried all the way to the airport. We waved as you drove away in the taxi. We stood out in the street waving until we couldn't see the car anymore.

Every time I take the lift up to our apartment, the little ding at every floor reminds me of the last time you came to visit us. I stood in the doorway and heard you coming up. I was so impatient. I couldn't wait to see you. *Ding. Ding.* It took forever. Then I saw your shining smile, and the joy bubbled up in me. There you were.

Today I began to write. I've named the file *Carl's Book*. I've written a little more than a page.

Those dim and blurry weeks.

I stick close to my beloved.

His warm hands.

His voice, his being.

Hands, voice, being.

The only thing my body acknowledges as

familiar, safe.

The only thing.

Him.

The only one.

My love.

Is just as big as my sorrow.

All the evenings we sat in a dark corner close together on
a crate and a rickety chair, talking and drinking wine. You
and me. You and me in the sorrow corner. We didn't turn on
the lights. We wanted to sit in a humble place in the house,
surrounded by old patio furniture, bags of withered leaves, we
wanted the darkness. We cried, we talked about our Carl. We
talked about the other children, we talked about our lives. We
talked about what had changed our lives. We held each other's
hands. This is how we got through that first year. I listened to
your breathing.

I breathe with you.

You breathe with me.

★

It's 22 September 2016 and I write:

In that stopped time, in this new time, in that time, consisting of the only moment that exists *right now*, no plans for the future can be made. None. Nearly one and a half years have passed. It is no time. *No time.*

When you can't make plans, you can't envision the future. Or anything else. When imagination is not a possibility, you cannot write. To write is *to imagine*. To write is also to move through time, via writing. To *create* time. Present, past, future. To write fiction is to invent images and structures, events and emotions in time. Arranged in time. With time as a factor, the compositional force. Time links everything that's imagined. But now it's not possible. It's not possible for me to write about anything other than this no-time. It's impossible for me to imagine myself writing in the future. Where there used to be ideas for writing about this or that in the future, now there is only silence. There is no movement. There is only deathly silence. We share the deathly silence with our dead. This is how we end up in the same place as the dead. We are here. But we are also with the dead. It's not difficult at all. It happens completely by itself.

It's possible to live in that deathly silent moment. It's possible to function. It's possible to do the most necessary thing, to ensure your own and your children's survival. It's possible to earn a living, buy groceries, cook dinner, do the laundry. It's possible to laugh. It's possible to have a nice time. The shock no longer controls every single moment we experience. There are many things that now seem completely meaningless. There are many things we avoid. Parties. Small talk. Projects that, before, we'd take on because 'that's what you do' or because it's good for your 'career', 'networking', a 'future life', projects that might be 'exciting', we now say a flat-out no to. We cannot do those kinds of projects. Our refusal is not dramatic or sad or in any way emotional. It is not painful. With a quiet mind, hushed and white, we now say no.

★

I find a note you wrote in 2014 about *Adagio for Strings* by Samuel Barber. The piece is from 1936. It circles around the same melody. First it climbs and then it falls, as though the melody were running up and down stairs. Like a bow, an arch. Then a long pause. Then back to the melody, which finally stops and fades out in one long tone. Barber's use of time in this piece is what gives it its character. Throughout, he manipulates the base rhythm by changing the tempo, for example: 4/2, 5/2, 6/2 and 3/2. The tempo is subtly raised and lowered. The simple base melody, the repeated figures and patterns, change imperceptibly. I listen to the piece. I think about how you experienced the music. I think about how, in poetry, we also use figures; finding a path through the material, by using figures, we find the delicate balance between different levels and tones, which form the entire work. You write:

```
Adagio for Strings. Process:
Death, rebirth
To overcome an obstacle
Life's path - childhood
To transcend from one state to another
Love
On the beach after the accident
The new world's beauty
```

★

I think about my children every day. I have always thought about my children every day. Because one of them is dead, it does not mean that I think about him less often. Rather, it feels even more pressing to think about him. It feels urgent to turn myself *towards where he is*. In no-time. That is, towards death. I mean, in the opposite direction from where my other children exist: in chronological time.

I don't differentiate between my children. I love them all equally. To have several children gives an automatic experience of *democratic love*. Because one of my children is dead, it doesn't mean that I give up that democratic love. My love is the same. My love will always be the same.

I think about my dead child; his time and his life are folded into me. I gave birth to him. I must hold his death. I will continue to fight like a lioness for him. No one should wrong him. No one should forget him. Not as long as I am alive. I still protect him, I know him just as well as I know my living children.

It's a physical feeling:

He is inside me.

He is inside my body.

I bear his spirit in my body.

I bear him again inside my body.

As when he was in my womb.

But now I bear *his entire life*.

I bear your entire life.

★

It's just Marley's voice and Marley's guitar, like a psalm, my sons
with bowed heads, I look at Carl diminishing, his disappearing
body, his missing consciousness, he looks almost like a corpse now,
but the respirator still wheezes, pulling air into him, blowing it out,
the chest heaves and lowers mechanically, it's unbearable, I hold
his hand, but I can't manage it, I run out, I run down the hall
and fall into the arms of the first person I meet, I am dizzy, and
I sob in the person's embrace, what should we do, what should we
do, there's nothing we can do, but we still have to wait. We wait, we
wait, they wheel Carl down to test if he can be declared brain-dead
now, outside the sun is shining, we go down and buy coffee in the

cafeteria, we sit outside in the sun, several people arrive, friends, colleagues, we drink coffee, we close our eyes, letting the sun shine on us, almost a moment of relief, conversation, short laughter, how is it possible to laugh? We go back up again, sit in the waiting room, the doctor comes in, he looks stressed. Is everyone here now? he asks. No, we're missing Martin. Where's Martin? He's still outside. Go down and find him, says the doctor, and someone goes to find Martin, it takes an eternity, he had to move his car, something about parking, finally he comes, now we're all here, a very large group, the doctor comes in again, he stands up, he says: At 3:45 p.m. Carl Emil Heurlin Aidt was declared brain-dead. The doctor has tears in his eyes. I am terribly sorry, he says, and I begin to scream, hoarse and uncontrollably, I cry, everything goes to pieces in that moment, someone is holding me, I've stood up and am about to fall over, everything goes to pieces, and they've rolled Carl away and now he's waiting for surgery, many are crying, Martin's face is completely white and frozen, my husband's face cracks, my mother's, my sister's, my children's, everything goes to pieces, as if until now there had been hope, but we knew there was never any hope, and yet there's a difference between him breathing and someone now about to turn the respirator off, so immense, so banally immense, it's the difference between living and dying, and the doctor calls Martin and me out into the hall again, I'd like to ask you, he says, if maybe you'd consider also donating some of his skin? Maybe his knees? And I say: His knees? Will you cut off his knees? Will you flay the skin off him? And the doctor says: No, we won't cut off his knees, we won't flay his skin, and the doctor smiles, we'll just take the meniscus from the knees and a little skin to the burn unit. And Martin and I say: No, we will not donate his skin and knees, you may not take any more from his body. Okay, says the doctor, that's fine, we don't need any skin at the moment, and then he goes, and we return to the waiting room, there's nothing more we can do here,

Carl will be operated on, and then they will turn off the respirator, and then he'll lie there all night alone in what they call the 'six-hour room', his dead body will lie alone in a dark room all night, and it makes me sick to think about it, I want to be with him, we want to be with him, but we can't, we're not allowed to, because tomorrow he'll be taken to the Forensic Institute, where he'll have an autopsy, but first he'll be cut open so they can remove his organs, then he'll be patched up, then he'll be cut open again for the autopsy, and patched up again, this body, my child's body, has to be exposed to so much, so much violence, his body, which is already completely wrecked, will be again and again wrecked even more, we gather our things and go, we go, we leave the hospital, we're a large group of people, barely able to put one foot in front of the other, we go out into the sunshine, we leave Carl.

It is 16 March 2015, and Carl is dead.

NOTES

The Rilke quote on page 7 is from 'Tenth Elegy', translated from the German by Stephen Mitchell (*Duino Elegies and Sonnets to Orpheus*, Vintage International, 2009).

The quotes by Walt Whitman on pages 23–4 and 25 are from his poem 'Song of Myself' (*Leaves of Grass: The 'Death-bed' edition*, The Modern Library, 1993).

'I'm loaded with bullets, no one should come to me with their soft shit' on page 28 is the author's paraphrase of a line by Ursula Andkjær Olsen in *Udgående Fartøj* (*Outbound Vessel*, Gyldendal, 2015).

The quote on page 97 is from Walt Whitman's poem 'When Lilacs Last in the Dooryard Bloom'd', (*Leaves of Grass: The 'Death-bed' edition*, The Modern Library, 1993).

Quotes from Stéphane Mallarmé's *A Tomb for Anatole* (North Point Press, 1983) on pages 30, 35, 38-9, 42, 44–5, 73–4, 115 and 127 are translated from the French by Paul Auster.

Quotes from Jacques Roubaud's *Some Thing Black* (Dalkey Archive Press, 1990) on pages 31, 63, 64, 65, 69, 86, 103, 112, 113, 114, 115 and 116 are translated from the French by Rosmarie Waldrop.

Quotes by Anne Carson on pages 37, 73 and 83 are from *Nox* (New Directions, 2009).

The quote from Plato's 'Phaedo' on page 40 is translated from the ancient Greek by Hugh Tredennick and Harold Tarrant (*The Last Days of Socrates*, Penguin Books, 2003).

Quotes by Emily Dickinson on pages 43 and 50 are from *The Gorgeous Nothings*, edited by Jen Bervin and Marta Werner (New Directions, 2013).

The quote by Jan Kochanowski on page 46 is from *Laments* by Jan Kochanowski, translated from the Polish by Seamus Heaney and Stanislaw Baranczak (Faber & Faber, 1995).

The quotes on pages 46–7 and 112 by Inger Christensen are from *Butterfly Valley: A Requiem*, translated from the Danish by Susanna Nied (New Directions, 2003).

The poems on pages 119–20 and 121 by the author are translated by Susanna Nied and Denise Newman.

The C. S. Lewis quotes on page 52 and 58 are from *A Grief Observed* (HarperCollins, 1994).

The quote by Ásdís Sif Gunnarsdóttir on page 56 is from her poem, 'Feminine Ways'.

The quotes from Hans Christian Andersen's story 'The Story of a Mother' on pages 70–1 are translated from the Danish by Jean Hersholt (The Hans Christian Andersen Centre, *The Complete Andersen,* available online).

Quotes from *Gilgamesh* on pages 77–8 and 96 are translated from the Assyro-Babylonian by Stephen Mitchell (Simon & Schuster, 2004).

Quotes from Denise Riley's *Time Lived, Without its Flow* are on pages 86–7, 92–3, 108–9 and 126 (Capsule Editions, 2012).

The Hipponion Text on page 111 incorporates phrases from the translation from the ancient Greek found on this site (*Harper's Magazine,* Browsing: The Harper's Blog, 5 December 2010, available online).

Definitions and encyclopedia entries are excerpted from Oxford English Dictionary, Webster's *New World Dictionary, Merriam-Webster Dictionary and Wikipedia, and translated from Ordbog over det danske sprog, Store medisinske leksikon* and *Den store danske encyklopædi.*

The lyrics by Bob Marley on page 119 are from his song 'Redemption Song'.

The quote by Nick Cave on pages 100–1 is from his documentary *One More Time With Feeling* (2016).

A heartfelt thanks to Line Knutzon, who ensured our survival during the first six weeks.

Thanks to my Danish editor, Simon Pasternak, who patiently helped me edit this book.

Thanks to everyone who has helped and supported me, accommodated me, talked to me, and written to me, before, during and after writing this book.

Special thanks to:

My huge family

The grieving group

Mette Moestrup

Denise Newman
Susanna Nied
Mieke Chew
Pejk Malinovski
Pia Juul
Helle Helle
Jakob van Toornburg
René Jean Jensen
Anders Abildgaard
Harald Voetmann
Ditte Channo
Pernille Fischer Christensen
Kim Fupz Aakeson
Nicole Carney
Jason Shure
Mindy Goldstein
Sine Plambech
Maria Vinterberg
Mia Steensgaard
Mette Mortensen
Lulla Forchammer
Shuki Foighel